Coaching Football Like A Basketball Coach

Kenny Simpson

DEDICATION

While there are many people that have helped me along my path as a Coach, there has been one that has had more influence on me that anyone else. That person is my wife, Jamey. She has not only been an encourager, but when needed she has kept me very level headed with not only my career, but in my personal life. I would never be in the place I am now had we never met and I am eternally grateful that God blessed me with a great wife.

"A wife of noble character who can find? She is worth far more than rubies. Her husband has full confidence in her and lacks nothing of value. She brings him good, not harm, all the days of her life."
Proverbs 31:10-12

"Coach Kenny Simpson has scored another touchdown with his book. Outstanding read that will help any coach grow and improve. Great wisdom and insight in relating football coaching to basketball."

Tim Horton, Running back coach Vanderbilt University

"This is a dynamite read! Coach Simpson has taken a unique look at coaching football by learning from another sport: basketball. As I read this book, I was really inspired to think more deliberately about football teaching methods. I enjoyed his take on "As football coaches we do XYZ, but basketball coaches do ABC." He then goes on to explain those differences, while at the same time making football coaches critique their own practice "why's and how's." I think this is tremendous offseason reading as coaches evaluate themselves and their practices."

Chris Fore, Eight Laces Consulting, California Coaches Association President

"Coach Simpson is a class act. He is always connecting and trying to help coaches. Coach takes a fresh approach with this new book and it's a slam dunk".

Shea Monroe, Alabama Spread and Defense Clinic

"Coach Simpson has done it again! This book challenges football coaches to become more dynamic in their approach to teaching the game. Coaching "concepts over plays" will allow coaches and players to have a deeper understanding of their playbook and how it can be used in every situation."

Brent Morrison, Head Football Coach at Westerville Central High School, Ohio

"Coach Simpson's book should be on every young coach's reading list regardless of scheme or style. It's a valuable resource to any football coach in today's game."

Kevin Swift, AD/Former Head Football Coach Gold Beach High School, Oregon

"Coach Simpson has a proven track record of coaching success in two states. I've watched him continue to grow and flourish as a head coach through the years."

Eric Cohu, Head Football Coach Little Rock Christian Academy, 5A State Champions (2018) and Former Head Football Coach at Madison Academy, Alabama.

"Coach Simpson has done a great job of running a program from top to bottom and is running an offensive system that enables his players to perform at a high level. He has put Batesville Southside football on the map here in Arkansas."

Tommy Gilleran, Head Football Coach Lake Hamilton

"Coach Simpson coached my two daughters at Alabama Christian Academy. Kenny had a positive lasting impact on both my daughters that will last a lifetime. He has spent a career encouraging student athletes to be the best they can be not only on the fields of play, but most importantly in life. Kenny is a great husband, father and coach in that order."

Brent Barker, Athletic Director Eagle Mountain Saginaw ISD and Former Athletic Director at Faulkner University

"I have coached against Kenny for several years in conference play and his teams are always well prepared and play with great effort. The program that he has built is one that consistently competes for the conference championship."

Tommy Shoemaker, Head Football Coach Central Arkansas Christian (2008-2019) and former Head Football Coach Harding Academy (1997-2007). Coach Shoemaker has 10 conference titles and 1 state championship.

Introduction

Like many high school football coaches, I had a unique path to becoming a Head Football Coach. As a young man growing up I had a passion for all sports, or any games for that matter. I just wanted the opportunity to compete. Throughout high school I was fortunate enough to be a part of 4 different sports (football, basketball, baseball and track) and I actually attended 3 different high schools as a military child. Needless to say, I was exposed to many different coaches and coaching styles during my upbringing. The opportunity to compete has always been something I have craved. I love how each sport has unique aspects and learning all the ways to use the rules to your advantage.

If it involves competition, count me in. While I was built more for baseball and track, I gravitated more to football and basketball. I also grew up when "focusing" on a sport would be laughed at. Due to this I've always enjoyed watching or playing almost any sport I was able to play. In my opinion, each sport compliments other sports. Skills you can acquire in basketball translate very well to football, just like skills from football can translate to other sports. We have seen the evolution of football over the past 10-20 years that is incorporating many "basketball" concepts.

My coaching career started at Madison Academy in Huntsville, Alabama where I was blessed to be a part of a state championship team (as a junior high coach) in basketball and a rebuilding football program. After 3 years of coaching both sports, I was able to take a defensive coordinator position at Alabama Christian Academy and after two years I was then a head coach at 27-years old. Despite not coaching basketball since that time, I have kept my love for the game and used many of the principles I used during my time coaching basketball with my football program. I have also been fortunate enough to coach track, and have loved my time in that sport as well. Coaching multiple sports has opened my eyes to many different techniques that can work between the sports.

While this book will focus on coaching football, I want to **highly encourage** all of those coaches in each sport to do your best to make sure your athletes know you want them to play multiple sports. Specializing is ruining youth athletics and I try to do my best to have athletes play as many sports as they can. If someone is asking an athlete to focus, they do not have that athlete's best interest in mind. Each year many people come out in support of all those multi-sport athletes, but each year we seem to find less and less athletes trying to play multiple sports. I feel often this is done by having "year-round" sports and I am personally very much against this. That includes football. As a coaching community I feel we must fight this growing epidemic.

Now to the premise of the book. This is not meant as a shot at football coaches, even "old-school" coaches. Football clearly is not basketball or baseball or any other sport. However, I believe the changes we are seeing in football have more to do with the use of space and the ability to "adjust" plays. This concept is seen easily through the game of basketball as it is a fluid game that requires adjustments each time up and down the court. We are starting to see many football programs embrace this concept in their own programs.

My goal in this book is to cause you to think of "why" you are teaching skills and drills to your players. And to cause you to know the "why" of your scheme and how it must be able to adjust. While I prefer my specific offense and defense, the goal of this book is to fit to any offense or defense. Take these principles, or concepts, and apply them to what you do in your program.

One of the top NFL athletes playing today is very pro multi-sport:

"And to me, I look at what basketball and track and baseball did for my football career -- it was more than anything -- you're training different muscles, you're training your mind, and just being a part of multiple teams you learn a lot of life lessons". Christian McCaffrey

This book will explore coaching football while using basketball principles. I hope to explain this more in detail in each chapter. During my time as a football coach I have clashed ideologically with several basketball coaches about the off season and specialization, but have always really enjoyed watching some great coaches teach their teams the way to be successful in basketball. In all sports, those coaches that are able to teach the fundamentals and have their team understand what they want to accomplish are going to be the most successful. However, in my experience basketball coaches that are great are experts at teaching the **concepts** of the game to their athletes, so they are able to make quick adjustments in the game and their team can execute them at a very high level. They are able to get their athletes to understand the game at a much deeper level than their opponents, and this allows their teams to function much quicker in all situations.

Lastly, before I get into all the X and O part of football, let me remind you that as a coach you have a great platform. Be careful with the words you use with your athletes.

Psalm 141:3 says, *"Set a guard, O Lord, over my mouth; Keep watch over the door of my lips."*

As I have become older, I have realized how impactful the words I use are to my players. If you coach long enough, you will have players come back to you and talk about stories from practice/games and what you have said. Many times I didn't even remember the details, but it made a big difference to these young men. I hope you gain something from this book, but always remember that we are molding young men and what you say will carry more weight than often what their own parents tell them. Be mindful that your words, good or bad, are often what shape how young men view themselves.

I've also coached a few players that are not with us anymore and often go back to thinking about what I may have been able to do differently that may have affected their lives in a more positive way. Remember that coaches impact more people's lives than almost any other profession, so take what you say seriously.

I'm hopeful this book may teach you one or two ideas that may help you along your coaching journey. I've been blessed to have worked for some of the best coaches in many sports. Great coaches are great coaches, no matter what sport they coach. Just like great teachers are great coaches. If you can reach young people and motivate them, you can be an excellent coach. The rest of coaching is work ethic and the ability to pass information on to your athletes. Best of luck in your coaching journey, and I hope you gain something from this book.

Forward

In 2009 I became the head boy's basketball coach at Alabama Christian Academy in Montgomery, Alabama. Kenny Simpson was the head football coach at ACA when I arrived. I even had a chance to coach Kenny's younger brother, Kirk. We worked together for several years while the Simpsons were in Montgomery.

Kenny, unlike some other football coaches I had worked with, took a real interest in the basketball program. We shared several multi-sport athletes and this working relationship was truly a blessing. I knew Kenny had played and coached basketball and genuinely enjoyed the sport. As a basketball coach in Alabama, this was truly refreshing. We pulled for each other's teams while working together.

I am currently an Athletic Director at a large public school district in Arkansas. I see the value that coaches, in all sports, bring to today's young people. Kenny and I share the vision of a coach who helps young people use sports as a way to overcome life's struggles, learn how to work with others, and a way to teach values that will help young men become good employees, husbands, and fathers.

I grew up in a small town in Arkansas. I remember going to watch high school football and basketball games as a young boy. The week's highlight was getting to go to the high school football and basketball games. I couldn't wait to run out on the field on Friday night as a Mena Bearcat. The sounds of the crowd, the smell, and the importance to the community were undeniable. It was the biggest event in town.

I always knew that I wanted to be a coach. Which sport, I wasn't sure, because I was a three-sport athlete in high school. I played football, basketball, and baseball. I probably enjoyed them, in terms of playing the sports, in that order. Although, I ended up playing collegiate baseball. When it came time to decide which sport would be the one I focused on as a coach, it came down to which sport would be the most enjoyable to practice every day. My choice ended up being basketball for that very reason. Practices were the most like a game. At least, that had been my experience.

I have been very fortunate to have coached many successful basketball teams in my career, including a number of conference championships and two state championships. I am proud of the fact that I was able to coach at pretty much every level of basketball. I started out as a junior high head coach then went on to become a high school head coach, college assistant, and college head coach. I cherish the memories of all the teams I coached over the last 28 years.

As I eluded to earlier, back 1980's Mena, Arkansas, I loved Friday night football. It was my first love. I was fortunate to start for three years in the defensive secondary. Football, at that time was all about toughness and execution. I loved it, but practices were long and monotonous. Games were great, but practices were just about survival. I think this is why we were known as a hardnose football program, but it is also the reason why I chose to become a basketball coach. I loved the fast-paced action of basketball practice.

As you read this book, I think you will find it applies to today's football game in so many ways. Kids today enjoy the fast-paced action of today's offenses. As I observe football practices today, many of them look like the practices I ran while coaching basketball. Quick, fast paced, with little or no down time. Also, the basic concepts taught in basketball help players succeed on the offensive and defensive ends of the floor. I think this is a great way to teach the game of football as well. Players need to understand what it takes to be successful on both sides of the ball. Kenny does a great job of writing about coaching football like a basketball coach.

Derek Harrell

Athletic Director – Marion High School

TABLE OF CONTENTS

Acknowledgements

When you do accomplish pretty much anything in life it is due to the great support system that is set up. No man is an island, and I am definitely a product of those around me. There is no way I can thank all the people in my life that have helped me to achieve many of the smaller goals I have set, but I do want to thank all those who have helped me become a follower of Christ and have guided me along the path.

There are several ladies in my life that have had a huge impact and this book is not an exception. My mother, Kathy Simpson has always been my biggest encourager from a young age and she continues in that role today. I've also been blessed to have a mother-in-law, Kay Jones, who is not only a great support for our family, but took the time to edit this book.

In addition to the ladies that have had an impact on my life, I've been blessed with a father that provided for our family. Many young men don't have the blessing of knowing their dad and I am probably closer with my father now than even when I was growing up. I have also been blessed with three brothers and a sister that have been very supportive of me.

Military men go underappreciated in our country and I am very proud of my Father, Father-in-law, Grandfather and Brother's service to our country. All of these men make me very proud of them.

I have also been very blessed because of some great head coaches that took a young coach who already had all the answers and slowly taught him that he didn't even know what he didn't know. Since becoming a head coach, I have started to appreciate them even more. Thank you Matt Clouser and Gregg Baker for giving me the opportunity.

Thank you to the Searcy School District for giving me the opportunity to lead a great football program. The administration, parents, community and most importantly, the kids, have been a blessing. I get to live everyday not ever having to "work" in such a great environment.

Thank you to Southside School District for having the faith in me to come in and lead our football program and sticking with me through some rough rebuilding seasons. Finding people that are loyal to a Football Coach is rare, and I am forever grateful to Roger Rich, Roger Ried, George Sitkowski and

Dion Stevens for their support.

I have been blessed to have worked with some of the best assistant coaches one can have. Many of them are now leading their own programs, or soon will be. A head coach must have a great staff if they are going to have any chance to be successful, and I have been blessed to work with some great men of character. I can be difficult to work with at times, but these assistant coaches are some of the best men I've been around.

Finally, I have been a witness to watching some of the finest young men during my time as a coach. If you played football for me, I continue to keep you in my prayers and am very proud to have seen some great feats on the field, but more importantly I've been able to see some young men grow into the leaders of many communities and families. Each team I have been around has been special to me and those relationships do not go away.

Think Like a Basketball Coach

"It's not what the coach knows; it is what his players know that counts"

-- Anonymous

I am very much a fan of the game of football. In my opinion it is the greatest sport that is played today in terms of teaching young men character, discipline and toughness. I think football has more than likely helped more young men get through high school than most would like to give it credit for, and it teaches many of the skills we want to pass on in our society. Football also is unique in that it requires unselfishness, as it is the only sport that does not allow each player to actually touch the ball. It is designed to make the team that plays together the most successful.

All of this being true, I have found that most of the best coaches in football share quite a bit in common with coaches of other sports, specifically basketball.

Basketball, is also a great sport and requires the ability to adapt and constantly make subtle changes. While basketball has several set "plays", it relies much more on the ability to constantly adapt and take advantage of matchups. Because the game moves so quickly, players must be able to adapt to many different situations each time down the floor on both offense and defense. This forces basketball coaches to teach **concepts** not just plays or sets. Teams that are great at basketball are able to quickly make minor adjustments on the fly, because they understand fundamental skills at a high level.

In this book I plan to use the word **concept** as, teaching your athletes not only fundamentals and plays, but teaching them to understand why something is done. By understanding why, they will know how it can be successful. Understanding the WHY will also allow them to make adjustments to an opponent. Basketball, due to the nature and pace of the sport, seems to be the sport that teaches this idea more than most other sports. Having players that understand **concepts**, allows many teams to beat those with superior athletes. Many times in football I have watched teams that can run 20 different coverages or plays, but they blow coverages or blocking schemes, because they don't understand the **concept** of what they are trying to accomplish. Many times those same teams struggle to adapt to their opponent or the situation in the game.

In my opinion the best coaches in football today think like the best basketball coaches. They look for the simple **concepts** and work very hard to be great at the subtle parts of the game. They both are great at the fundamentals, but have players that understand why they are so important. Both sports work hard to coach the situations of the game. Football has plenty of situations that must be understood to be successful and I will delve into some of these in later chapters, but basketball seems to have a new situation almost every possession. All great teams must be able to adapt constantly.

Having players that understand concepts, allows many teams to beat those with superior athletes. Many times in football I have watched teams that can run 20 different coverages or plays, but they blow coverages or blocking schemes, because they don't understand the concept of what they are trying to accomplish.

The problem with Assuming

My problem has always been as a coach that I make the assumption that my assistant coaches and players know what I'm thinking. As I have gained more and more experience, and learned the hard way often, I have started to "over-communicate". Make sure your coaches know what your theory is in as many situations as possible. Many assistant coaches may still be learning the nuances of the game and simply don't know what you expect. I want to make sure we go over as many details as possible during film/team periods. We want our kids to focus on fundamentals during "individual" and "group" time. But we want to focus on situations during our film time and our team periods.

As we have moved forward we have started to make sure any time we are in "team" we always have a situation. The obvious ones are down and distance, but it has amazed me how many times on 3rd/4th down our kids would commit "bad" penalties in practice. As a coach, we must be constantly mindful that not all of our athletes watch our sport on TV, or grew up playing. It is always better to repeat something multiple times than to have one athlete not be aware of situational football.

Some simple situations need to be focused on for example — Penalties we never want to commit: off-sides on 3rd and short, pass interference short of the sticks on 3rd/4th down. We want to make sure our guys do that in practice, so we can teach it out of them before we play a game. Time management can be key to many wins in close games. We have often gone 2-for-1 at the end of the half with teams by scoring to close the half and beginning with the ball to start the 2nd half. Our athletes understand this is a major goal for us.

Football is a game that is often won and lost on knowing the situation, and we want to make sure our kids understand the larger concept. I will go in detail more about this in later chapters, but having athletes that understand the game at even a decent level will help you much more than getting an extra 5-10 minutes of simply running plays or running drills. Football games are not simply running plays, but they are understanding the situation and **concept** of your offense in that situation. Make sure you are practicing these concepts every day.

Where Basketball Coaches Do Well

These are the areas of football that I feel get neglected by many coaches (myself included), whereas many basketball coaches seem to do a great job of focusing on:

1) Fundamental skills that translate into the game

*"Success is neither magical nor mysterious. Success is the natural consequence of consistently **applying** the basic fundamentals."* - Jim Rohn

The key word is applying. Too many times I watch coaches run drills and they think that takes care of the fundamental skill set. This is NOT the case. Any coach has fundamental drills they run pretty much every day. We teach each position specific drills and we work them often. Fundamentals are the key to being a great football team. However, just because you work a drill does not mean it will help you win. If the athlete cannot take that drill and apply it to an actual game situation, you are wasting your time.

Problems I see with "drills" we run

It wasn't until I became a head coach that I began

to notice all the worthless drills we tend to run as football coaches. I am not saying the drill serves no purpose, just saying that the drill may not have anything to do with what we are trying to accomplish on offense. There are times for very many different drills, and I love to explore different drills as a coaching staff. Some drills may also have a great purpose for one staff, but don't really fit with what another program is doing.

For example — I've seen routes being run with our running backs that we have no intention of ever running in a game. I've seen us working tip drill every day with our defensive backs. There is nothing wrong with either of these drills, but as a coaching staff you must ask, "Is the time being invested in this ever going to impact the actual game?" We are a Shotgun Wing-T team, so we don't spend much time on max protection drop back passes on years we don't plan to run that much. In short, make sure you are spending your practice time wisely on what is going to help you win. There is nothing I hate more as a head coach than to watch a position group waste their time in individual on drills that will not help us win games.

I've also seen multiple drills that are great drills, but the players have no idea how this translates into a game situation. Drills are needed for each position, but with an explanation of why this drill helps us win football games. How does this drill look on the field on Friday night? Drills are great, but they MUST have a purpose.

Solution Idea

One of the things I have started doing, and I stole from some great coaches, is to ask my coaches what they'd do if they only got 5 minutes of individual, 10 minutes of individual, 30 minutes of individual time... When they answer that question you know what is prioritized and should be worked every day, every other day, once a week, or even mainly during the offseason. Make sure you treasure time in individual periods on the practice field.

Be sure to have your athletes fully aware of the purpose of the drill and the key points. Athletes want to be great on game days, and if they understand how this drill will help, they will give great effort

Also, be sure to have your athletes fully aware of the purpose of the drill and the key points. Athletes want to be great on game days, and if they understand how this drill will help, they will give great effort (the majority of the time). I've also found it great to video a drill and have it watched with their position coach. Anything you video and watch is much easier to correct, and although we are limited on time throughout the season, it is great to do this early and explain the drill, so as you move forward, your athletes understand the reason we run it. Better to spend a little extra time at the beginning of the season to get a drill done right, than to have lots of bad habits being formed and need to be corrected later.

2) Teach the situations in the game

> "We try to stress the little things, because the little things lead to big things" -- Steve Alford

Watching games in all sports I am amazed at the mistakes made by very good (and very well coached) teams in critical situations. Most of the time as a coach we understand what is going on in the game and the situations, but as is often proven on the field, our players don't know the situations as well as we do. A very smart older coach once told me, "I don't care what you know, I care what your players know since they are the ones that win and lose the game". Be sure to teach the situations to your team. It sounds almost elementary, but be sure your athletes understand the fundamental rules of the game - down and distance, time management, etc.

One thing basketball coaches have to work on all the time, because they play so many games, is how to handle end of the game situations. How many times have you seen a team take a foul on purpose to slow the game down, or even let the other team score and avoid fouling? Understanding what to do at the end of a game is an art, and the great coaches know how to handle it. Football coaches that are very successful also understand the larger picture and how to handle situations to give their team the best opportunity to win.

I have seen some very prepared football teams that do work the odd situations of the game, so their players are prepared and are as detail oriented as to coach up many of the parts of the game that so often get under-coached. Here are just a few areas that I am talking about when I mention the situations in the football game that come up more often than we realize:

A) Working from the Hash Marks in High School football

I can vividly remember looking up one time to see my safety almost standing on top of one of my cornerbacks on defense and wondering why in the world they wouldn't figure out that was probably not the best alignment. I had never bothered to get into the reasons with our defense as to why an offense might align tighter when they have ⅔ of the field to work with. I called a timeout and we quickly had a discussion that should have happened a long time before that play. I have been around some great coaches that have coached up their defense/offense into how to use the field to their advantage. But more often than not, I see many teams that play the game as if every snap was from the middle of the field, specifically on defense.

I don't want to get into a bunch of our specifics, but we now work our script on offense at least once a week to go from left hash, middle of the field, right hash in a rotation to at least work this with our play calls. I tell the players before the period why we are doing this and we obviously will work our alignment on offense now. We have started doing this more and more with our defense and paying attention to where the most "grass" is for an offense. I'd highly recommend at least working this into your team period, if not anywhere else on your schedule and making sure your athletes understand how their role may change depending on the field.

B) Running plays against the clock

I would think most teams work a two-minute drill with their offense. Most teams also work a four-minute drill, working on wasting the clock. This is not a new idea for football coaches. Make sure your players are aware of what stops the clock and what keeps the clock moving. This sounds very common and it should be known, but I have found that it must constantly be reinforced.

What I am referring to in this section is very specific situations:

1-20 seconds left with no timeouts and we are down X.

2-Working we must score a touchdown on this play.

3-Coming out of your own endzone when you must run the clock out

4-Transitioning from offensive personnel groups or from offense to kicking game

Be sure to also work these situations on defense. Teach your athletes when only a touchdown will beat you or that you must get a team out of field goal range or force a turnover during practice each week will make sure you are prepared for when this happens in a game. I have to make sure I script to work all these game situations at the beginning of a season and follow this or it is easy to not have prepared.

C) 3rd down plays

This is the situation games are won and lost in my opinion. More games come down to who can keep possession of the football than almost any other statistic. Very well coached teams may not always convert 3rd downs, but they are always aware of where the first down is. Think about how many times as a coach, that you have witnessed a player be completely unaware of the down and distance. We work a third down period every day when we have team offense.

The great teams also are sure to work 3rd downs on defense. We have taught our defensive backs when and where it would be acceptable to commit pass interference. In our state, it is not an automatic 1st down and we are sure to make our defenders aware of this. We also teach our defense to defend the sticks and discuss all the potential blitzes we will use. This sounds extremely elementary, but remember on the field it is not 11 coaches playing the game, it is 11 young men than must be able to understand the situation of the game. I have often told my coaches we are not trying to out-scheme the other coach, we just have to out-scheme the 16-year old player on the opposing team. So, be sure you are teaching your players the situations of the game.

D) Two-point plays or 4th down plays

For us as an offense all the rules change on two-points plays, and often on 4th down plays (depending on the time in the game). We want to make sure our players are aware that now we don't prize taking care of the ball, or making the "smart" football play. Often times we want our QB to throw the ball up for grabs and look to extend plays with his legs in the backfield. We also work "fumbling" the ball into the end zone if we are going to be tackled short of the line to gain.

The same principles must be taught to our defense. We also discuss that we are willing to try to "time up the snap" if we think it is needed in specific situations. We also work on making sure our players are aware of where the 1st down marker is and how that will change our coverage some. On two-point plays we also coach our defenders that we want to be much more aggressive in coverage or in blitzes as if it were 4th and goal. It was surprising to me how many times I'd watch our athletes in practice line up inside the endzone and backpedal, before we were able to correct it.

E) Special Teams situations

Many teams will do this on Thursday or on Monday, but we want to try to be very specific each time we run a special team. If we are working our Punt Team, we want to work coming out of our endzone, or pinning the other team deep inside the 20. We work our kickoffs to the dead zones of the return team as well as onside kicks. We work our return for if the ball lands in different spots on Kickoff Return. We want to make sure we have covered what this team will look like in a game situation. Be sure to cover with your punt and field goal block teams what to do if the ball is blocked. We teach never falling on the ball. We also go over what to do if the ball is blocked and move to our side of the field. Be prepared in all special team situations and you will be surprised how many times you will win this area of the game.

F) 2nd and "shots"

I'm sure many teams look at 2nd and short as a chance to go down the field and be very aggressive, but how many teams coach their players how you expect this situation to play out. It took me until the first time I had a quarterback take a sack on 2nd and 1 to figure out that I needed to at least make him aware of what we were doing. Once our quarterbacks understood these were "shot" plays they were much more consistent in checking for the play and then throwing the ball away.

In the same way when scouting an opponent many times you can find their shot plays and when they like to run them. Be sure that your athletes are aware of when these will take place. You cannot always be perfect on your predictions, but most teams are teams of habit.

3) Defending the other team/player not simply using your "system"

"If we fail to adapt, we fail to move forward". -- John Wooden

I will cover this in another chapter, but this is something we want to be sure that we do as a staff. I've heard several coaches make the reference, "make them beat you left handed" in basketball. Basically, we are going to force you to beat us with someone else or make your best player do what we feel he doesn't want to do.

Too many times I've watched teams get shredded by a player on the other team and they never adjust. They simply run whatever "rules" their defense dictates. Our defense will always have built in flexibility to at least make a team beat us with their other players. In basketball you see teams do this by double teaming a player and forcing the ball out of his hands — and they only have 5 players! If basketball coaches can do it, then football should be able to do it much easier with 11 guys to work with. I've lost my share of games over my career, but we always wanted our players to know who their best athlete is.

4) Making very quick in game adjustments

"The most incredibly interesting thing about being a leader is what adjustments you make and how you make them while keeping your core principles alive and well". -- Mike Krzyzewski

The game of basketball is such an up-tempo game that coaches are forced to work the adjustments almost every possession. They must see the game as it is going and make adjustments almost instantly. In football the game is fast, but it is much more specialized with offensive and defensive players and is played at a slower pace, which should make adjustments even easier to make. However, it is also much harder to see the nuances that happen, since it involves so many more players.

Making adjustments has become the key to our program's growth over the last few seasons. We now spend time at the TV or IPAD between each possession and make very quick adjustments to what isn't working. For this to be successful, your staff must practice what to do and what to look for in the middle of a game. Which coaches look at which spots? How do you communicate this to two-way players? How do we run this through the head coach? If you don't have a plan on how to use technology, it will be of no benefit to you or your program and will actually cause more harm than good.

Most coaches are very willing to make adjustments in game, but often we have not done the groundwork for how we will do this. As a head coach you must empower and equip your assistant coaches to make adjustments. Obviously, as a head coach I want it communicated to me, and I will have the final decision, but make sure you practice this. This also goes with personnel decisions that need to be made. Each team comes in with a depth chart and an idea, but often adjustments must be made as injuries occur. Any ground work you can set before the game begins, and practice before the actual game happens will greatly benefit your program. You can plan for as many scenarios as you want, but what makes sports great is the unexpected so you must have your staff ready, just like you want your players ready to make adjustments.

As a head coach you must empower and equip your assistant coaches to make adjustments.

If you are going to be successful you must have built in adjustments (I will talk more about these in the next few chapters), but you must also be willing to make changes from possession to possession. I have heard it said, "At the high school level teams make adjustments the next game, college coaches make adjustments the next half and NFL coaches make adjustments the next series", but I'd challenge you as a coach to make them quickly and decisively. I feel great coaches make adjustments instantly because they understand their concepts to the point that they can anticipate what the opponent is going to attempt to exploit. Have a game-plan and plan of attack, but you also need to be prepared to make the needed changes during a game.

While this book is about thinking like a basketball coach, often football is a much more difficult sport to coach due to all the moving parts and positions. Having a great system set up will allow you to be successful in both sports, but in football you must work to have a great staff that is an extension of you to your players. Be sure that you have spent the needed time with you staff, and they understand your expectations in practice and in games. One area I always feel I neglect until we work through a few scrimmages is how we will communicate on the sideline with coaches and with two-way players. Make sure you work several dry-runs before you get into a real game.

Football is a great sport, but there is a reason most successful programs have multiple coaches on staff. You cannot be a great football coach or have a successful team unless you are also coaching your assistants to be an extension of you. Be sure to lay out clear expectations and then empower them to be great, just like you should with your players.

Concepts > Plays - Offensive Edition

"Our job is not to prepare students for something. Our job is to help students prepare themselves for anything." - A.J. Juliani

Let me explain the idea of a "concept" and not a "play". To me a **concept** is something that is much larger than simply learning a play. Anyone with a whiteboard can draw up a pass play that the WRs can follow, and the blocking scheme is set. **Concepts** have built in answers to what the defense may give you. When you are teaching **concepts,** you are allowing players to understand more than just the basics of play/blitz/coverage. You are teaching them why this works and how to make adjustments. Plays are easy to teach, just like teaching kids for one test. Teaching **concepts** is a much deeper and longer lasting impact on

The dictionary defines a concept as a mental abstraction which allows generalization and the extension of knowledge from some known objects to others unknown. It integrates two or more particulars into a common mental unit. Basically this is teaching players how to take what you are teaching them and adapt these fundamentals into all situations they may face as a player.

athletes.

Basketball coaches teach **concepts** all the time, as they have to work against multiple different looks on most possessions. Taking this over to football, I want my players to understand our basic plays and how we can adapt them with simple adjustments. This takes them understanding your offense and your philosophy. They must also be able to take their fundamental drills and quickly translate them into a team setting.

In the run game they include the following:

1) RPO built into the play
2) Counter play that looks the same
3) Play Action Pass of the same action
4) Different adjustments to the blocking scheme that are subtle, but effective

In the passing game a concept has the following:

1) Built in adjustments to the routes
2) Ability to switch routes with WRs/RBs
3) Ability to run the same concept from MULTIPLE formations
4) Easy, clear reads for the QB

Teaching a **concept** is all about making sure your athletes know:

1) What you are trying to accomplish

The idea of simply putting in plays because other teams run them and they seem to work is not the best approach to running an actual offensive system. Instead, you need to look at how this fits within what you are attempting to accomplish as an offense. Can you put in a play that you can run in all your offensive alignments? Does this play work against all the possible fronts you may see with some very slight adjustments? Can you hang your hat on this play? What will be your compliments to this play? All of these questions need to be answered instead of simply putting this in because it works for someone else.

After you have decided this is something for your offense, you now must explain to your athletes how this play will work and set up other parts. You should explain the intricacies of what that play needs. How we will adjust to different looks? Once your athletes understand this, the play needs to be run over and over again until they start to make adjustments on their own during the offseason. If your players understand how to make it work, it will have a much better chance at being successful.

The next level of teaching your **concept** is to show your athletes how teams will attack it on defense. What are they going to attempt to do to stop you? Teach your players what to expect so that when the time comes, you have answers already built in to your system. Most coaches have these already built in, but the great coaches make sure their athletes are aware of these.

Most teams simply scrap a play during a game that "doesn't work". We want to be able to make the adjustments so that our players understand that our system will work, no matter what the defense does. When your athletes understand the **concept** of the system, they can make adjustments or

The hard part for most coaches is to not put too much in your offensive system. Work hard to be great at what you do. Understand what adjustments and small tweaks you can make. You only have a certain amount of time in a season/practice, and you want to make sure that is going towards what you want to live with on offense.

recommend adjustments to your plays.

2) Why you are running a certain concept

Does this play mesh with your personnel this season? You need to understand the "WHY" of each concept you put in. The best years I have had as a coach were due to us adjusting our concepts to our players. One season we were built to run the ball and we simply worked on our 3-4 run concepts with small tweaks. We worked the play action and the screen game off these runs. Another season we needed to set up the run by having several screens and working more of the RPO game. All coaches are willing to make adjustments to their personnel, but at the high school level it must become a priority for the coaching staff.

If you understand why these concepts are successful, you will have a much better knowledge of what adjustments will be to not only what the defense is doing, but how to make it work with your athletes. My staff and I are big in the Wing-T concepts in running the ball. Because of this I visit with any coach that runs these concepts to gain as much knowledge as possible on the areas of what they do well. Sit down with these coaches that are experts and learn not just how, but why they believe in what they believe in. Take what you feel you can use in your system and with your athletes. Do not simply try to take what one successful program does and implement all of it into your system.

The hard part for most coaches is to not put too much in your offensive system. Work hard to be great at what you do. Understand what adjustments and small tweaks you can make. You only have a certain amount of time in a season/practice and you want to make sure that is going towards what you want to live with on offense. I have made the mistake many times of spending way too much time on a play or installing a new set on offense, and the cost of time was nowhere near the return I was hoping to gain.

On the flip side, we have also made many in game (or even in the middle of the drive) adjustments because our athletes understand simple concepts. We've changed pass concepts because the QB/WR would tell me what could be open off play action and did it the next drive. Those took literally zero time to install, because our athletes had been working on the routes and blocking scheme all year. The only players that knew this was a "new" play were the QB and the WR.

3) How defenses will attack this and what our answers will be for a concept

One of the best attributes a coach can have is understanding the weakness in any scheme. Defensive coordinators are going to probe to find what each type of offense struggles with. Get ready to see any kind of defense from week to week. On easy weeks I see the same look I've seen on film, but on many weeks we get a very different defense that is set to stop what we are trying to do. Also, be ready to see a repeat of a defensive front/coverage that you may have struggled with the previous weeks.

Offensively you MUST have answers for every look with the concepts you run. If you are a run heavy team, you need to have an answer for when they overload the box — It can be QB run, screens, play action, but it must fit within your system. If you are a team that throws it every down, you must have the answer for man press and blitzing. Whatever your concept is on offense, you need to be sure to build in answers. Not only do you need to know your answers, but you must explain it to your athletes as well. Their belief in the system is what will make all the difference. If they think we know what to do against anything that can be thrown our way, they will play with great confidence.

We spend probably ⅔ of our team practice time working situations and as I tell my offense, "worst case looks". I try to do most of this on Tuesday and early in our Wednesday practice so that our players understand what our answer will be if the defense is stopping our base packages. Make sure your players know what we may see and how we will adapt to the look we may get. While we want to get the look we expect the most, we want to be prepared for what could give us the most problems. I want Tuesday to be harder on the offense than Friday will be.

For example - Since we are heavy Wing-T formations, we see some defenses that put their best player attempting to jam up the strong side. We have 3-4 adjustments in how we will handle this that we have worked on all summer, but we remind our athletes EVERY Tuesday and work our adjustments, even if we don't think we will need them that week. We want to be prepared for the worst possible look and have our built in answers instead of working a bunch of new plays that week.

In whatever offense you run, be sure to work what you fear will cause you the most problems.

4) How this concept can work against ANY front or coverage

We want to get as much value for the time we invest in every **concept** as possible. I am willing to spend countless hours teaching the "Buck Sweep" because we feel the **concept** is more valuable than just a play. We can run Buck with about 10-15 adjustments off it, but for 9 of our 11 players it is the same. So the time spent is well worth it.

I understand that certain plays work better against certain looks, so I am not suggesting simply running a play and banging your head against a wall. Adjustments must be made all the time in any sport. What I am suggesting is having a **concept** that can work with small adjustments and having built in answers. In the Wing-T world these are known more as a "series" or having a play and 2-3 compliments off of the play. But in modern day football most people have simply added several RPO **concepts**. We want to merge the two and have other plays, but within the **concept** of the play we have built in answers also.

Most coaches I hear talk about having 200 plus plays actually have about 20-30 **concepts**, which is still way too many in my opinion, but they have subtle changes that we have already built in to our **concept.** Instead of running "36 counter G", we try to use one word concepts and then tag the player that can run the counter. Now we can run Quarterback Counter, Running Back Counter or even in our offense Wingback Counter. We can also tag a different puller if needed or have a "stay" call if we want to kick with our running back. This makes it look like 3-4 blocking schemes, but in reality is one **concept,** and since we have so few concepts, we are able to make the adjustments.

As football coaches, each of us have our own "system" or our way of getting plays called as well as formations. All of this is great and each coach needs to do this. There are plenty of styles of offense and all of them have seen success, so I am not advocating just a "style" or specific system of offense. This chapter will be about making all of your **concepts** as basketball coaches would see them as multiple ways to run the same play and multiple options off each play.

When designing an offense, I've heard many coaches boast about the number of plays they have or formations they can get into. I have no issue with this, but a basketball coach would consider most of these "new plays" as simply options off the original **concept**. For example, if a team runs inside zone and runs bubble screens off it, they would put it together — thus the RPO game that has revolutionized the game. I am not going to delve into the RPO world and get lost down that rabbit hole, although I am a huge fan of RPO's. Instead this book is a little more about the theory behind WHY people become creative on offense and is hoping to explain the thought process behind it.

Here is an example to show what I am talking about: in our offense we call "Snag" which is a chute route, corner route and curl route. Most offenses have this play, it is not new or inventive in any way.

Here it is diagramed below.

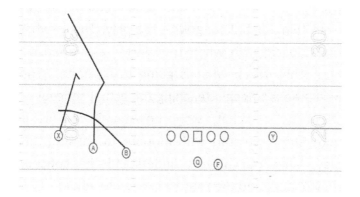

What we do with our athletes is to teach each of them the concepts of the play. What we are trying to accomplish with the play. How the defense can play if (man or zone). What the QB's reads are to the play. We want them to understand as much as possible (and we can put this time into the play since we only have "3 pass plays").

Once our kids understand the concept, we rep each route with each player that may run it. We teach the intricacies of the route vs different looks they may see. We teach the aiming points and how to get open in those. The main goal here is that our players understand how the routes may have slight changes due to zone, leverage, or man-to-man coverage.

The next step is we work our base play with no motion and become as good at this as we can. We will make sure it is right and understood before we even think of tinkering with the play. This is what most coaches do when they install any offensive play. They teach what is going to be done. The next step is to begin teaching the actual concept of the play — What, why, how... Once this is understood we start with motions to get into this play. Since our players understand the concept they understand the route will need to adjust.

Here is an example of a motion and adjustment to the same play.

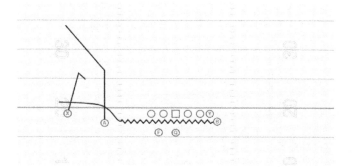

All we are doing with this is bringing the same player in what we call "bus" motion and running the exact same concept. Many teams are already doing this, but it makes it much tougher on a defense to go from a 2 x 2 set into a 3 x 1 set and will force teams to scout and spend time defending a play that once we have the concept built in takes us very little time in practice.

Here is another example.

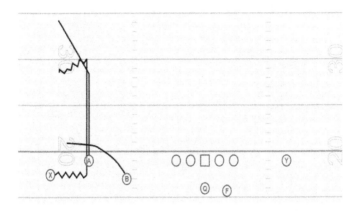

Again a very simple easy motion that we run with multiple plays, but it looks different for the defense and creates almost a "bunch" action for our team. This is something we do often against man-to-man teams, or if we are having a difficult time getting a free release from our outside WR. We simply teach that we want to "end our route" in the same place as we would if we had not come in motion, so the "X" will run almost a long hitch and work out.

The next thing we do is work our "switch concept". Now we are running the same concept but different WRs run the other routes. Here is an example of this.

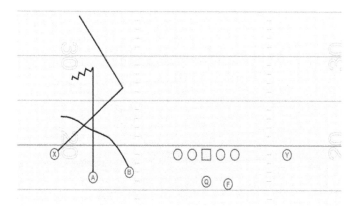

All we have done is run the same concept, except our "X" and "A" will **switch** responsibilities. "X" understands that he will need to bend his route in before running a corner route and "A" understand he needs to work to 10 yards and then work to the hole in the zone or work off his man if we are getting press coverage. Very easy read for the QB, since it is the same **concept** for his reads.

Often times we will run the same concept from a different formation. We run the same routes and the same **concept**, but from different areas on the field.

Here is an example of the same play from a slight formation adjustment.

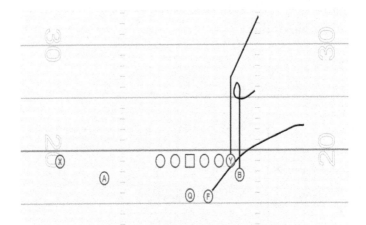

This is the same concept, but we would call it "snag strong," since it is to the strong side of the field. The route combination is the same and will work similar for the WRs as they have all learned the **concept**. Same reads for our QB as well.

The final part is when we add in our tags. We may tag a route to a player since the defense is over running the play (we also teach our players adjustments in base plays, but these are called by a coach to take a shot usually).

Here is an example of one of these.

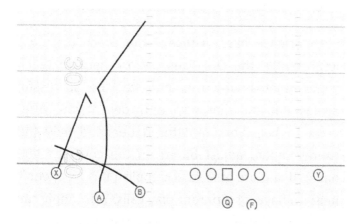

This is the same call for us, but we are "tagging" a player and a route. This would be "Snag, A COP". Generally, if we are doing this, it is because we are 90% sure we will throw the tagged route, so I'd highly suggest being sure you know it will come open. We can tag any player and a route that will attack the defense.

After we are done with this, our one concept has 30-40 different looks for the defense. We do this to each of our pass concepts. By the end of our offseason we will have 3 trips pass plays, 2 drop back passes (and 1 is verticals) and 4 quick game passes (2 WR routes). But when our kids understand how these plays work it is easy to make the adjustments. As a coach, the only limitation is your imagination. This allows us plenty of flexibility in our passing game, because we are simply working on what our foundation has allowed.

Each offense has a **concept** the coach (or more importantly, the QB) likes. Work hard to teach your athletes why this play can be successful against any look that may get thrown at you. Also, work to help your athletes understand how the routes should adjust based on the coverage you have. If you are able to accomplish this, you won't need to have 14 different play calls. You simply call the same play and the players understand what to do.

We want to give our linemen freedom to communicate at the line of scrimmage and make the correct calls so that they can get the defense blocked. If they understand what we are attempting to accomplish, they are able to make many adjustments on their own and can tell the coach why a play is not working. Many times, we've simply listened to what the linemen were suggesting.

Running Game

In our running game we are very similar with our plays. We are a wing-t based, gap scheme and use a lot of pin and pull in our run game. We work most of our base runs and teach our offensive linemen the same way we teach our WRs in the passing game. One season I realized that our linemen had no idea where the ball was going and what their main goal was. All they knew was to block down or pull. Making in-game adjustments was a nightmare.

From this point on, we wanted each of our players to understand the **concept** of each run play. If they understand they may "get beat", but simply can't "get beat" to one side or the other, they are able to block much more effectively. This also should minimize those terrible "away from the play" flags that drive coaches crazy. We teach a backside lineman that even though all blocks are important, the probability of a backside defensive player, who is already beat by alignment, making the play is very low. Don't ever hold on the backside of a play.

In high school football the offensive line is the difference between wins and losses. We want our linemen to know not only the scheme, but how teams will attack it and how to answer those attacks, so we start with letting them know the basic play. Here is buck sweep from our set.

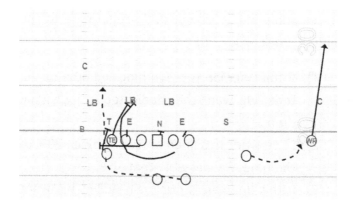

After teaching the basic rules and play, we work very hard to teach each position their base blocks, and drill the fundamentals every day. We work the blocks we will use most by each position at the same proportion they will use it — for example, a Strong Tackle in our offense will more than likely never pull, so he never works that in Individual time (he would double up on down blocking). Fundamentals are a must! Do not neglect teaching your guys the blocks they will use and the footwork they need. More importantly, don't forget to explain to them how the drill goes into the scheme.

Often times I've seen offensive line coaches work all their players equally on each block, and this is fine for some blocks or schemes. But we have linemen that are created differently and need to be used in different ways in our offensive scheme.

For example, we work our drills equal time to the type of block expected:

1) If this lineman is down blocking 50% of the time, we want that dedicated in individual time.
2) If we want this lineman to cut block 20% of the time, we will work that also.
3) If this lineman is our main puller, we want to work this the majority of his individual time.

Often times teams feel they must do a lot of "group" or "team" to accomplish this. I would much rather coach them up with 1 coach and a smaller group, and then bring it together for a shorter amount of time. We try to only run 10-12 plays during inside drill and 10-15 plays (pretty much all scenario work or motions/shifts) during team periods. Once the line understands the scheme and they know how to execute blocks, making adjustments in games are much more simple.

After working the fundamentals and base blocking we start to go over scenarios they may see. We don't take time to go over each and every situation, but use our rules as a base and give them potential problems they would see and how to handle them. We work how to "get beat" and still accomplish the block (example would be if you have to give up penetration be sure to turn defender inside). Make sure your line knows where the ball should go on all plays. Don't ever assume they know or understand.

Once the linemen all understand what we expect on each play, we begin to work tags for our reads and different ways to block at the point of attack. Here is an example of buck sweep again if we simply make the call for buck (or in our offense some other words).

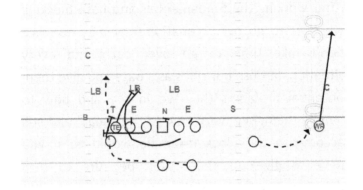

I don't want to get very specific, as this is not the point of the book, but this is our basic version of buck sweep. We have a one-word call for it, and our line and skill understand their basic rules. This would be installed on day 1 as it is our bread and butter play.

Here it is with our line making an adjustment ("Bypass" for our wing).

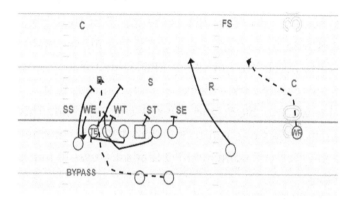

Simple line call when we are having issues with a very talented nine-technique inside our wing. Instead of abandoning the **concept**, we adapt the play and our athletes understand how it can look different.

We want to give our linemen freedom to communicate at the line of scrimmage and make the correct calls so that they can get the defense blocked. If they understand what we are attempting to accomplish, they are able to make many adjustments on their own and can tell the coach why a play is not working. Many times, we've simply listened to what the linemen were suggesting -- For example a double team vs. a free release — and have made that adjustment in game, or even in the middle of a drive.

We also marry each of our runs with our RPO concepts. I don't want to get into all of those, but feel free to contact me if you'd like more details. Pretty much, we run all our RPO game through who the backside tackle blocks. He has 3-4 calls that tell him who to block and the QB who to read. This again allows one run to look like 10 different ones and when you combine RPO reads it grows to many more.

Here are just a few tags we put with this base run that make our linemen's job much easier.

"STEAL" — The only player that needs to know anything on this is our backside tackle. This simply tells him to block the outside most defensive player, and our QB will read the defensive linemen.

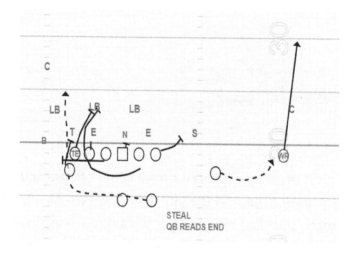

STEAL
QB READS END

Very easy adjustment for us to make against teams that are trying to take away buck sweep with the backside defensive tackle/end.

"FAST or NOW" — Only players that need to know how this works are the WRs. Most teams already run this and it is a simple compliment to any run on the backside.

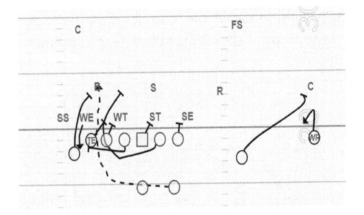

This is the simplest RPO we have in our offense and is usually a day 1 installation for us. We simply teach pre-snap leverage. Many teams run a similar concept and we like it because it forces the defense to become more balanced and defend the entire field.

"KEY" — This tells our QB to read the backside inside linebacker. It is a very easy read for the QB and requires no time for the offensive line.

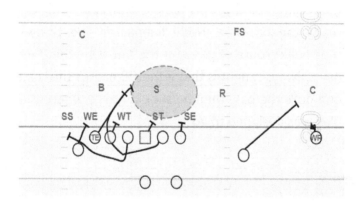

This is another simple adjustment for us to read another player on the defense. Our goal is to always have built in answers to any **concept** in our running game. The last thing we want to do is be forced to abandon our favorite run play and this gives us one more adjustment.

"PEAK" — We work this concept with our inside WRs on base passes as well, but then we often tag it with a run going the other direction. Many teams are running this simple concept. The QB reads the backside inside linebacker and throws the "peak" route or gives for the run. One thing we have always taught is that if the QB misses the read and pulls the ball, then he should run to where the play was designed to go.

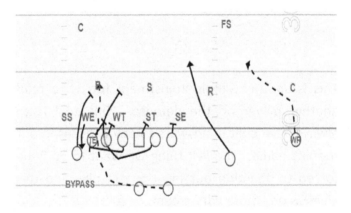

We put this in due to having a QB that was not as talented a runner, but was able to throw a very accurate ball and we wanted to still read the same player on the defense. Another simple concept for our WRs. We actually will run this same pass **concept** in other plays.

"STOVEPIPE" — Another simple term that only the backside tackle needs to know. This tells him to ignore the backside defensive end,, and try to climb to scoop a 2nd level player. The QB then will read the backside defensive end.

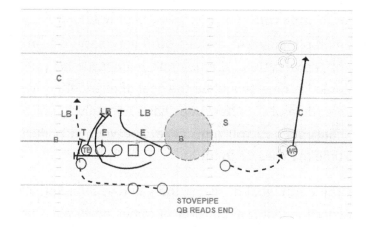

STOVEPIPE
QB READS END

Pretty self-explanatory read for our offense. It is just one more way to make sure we have answers to what the defense may bring.

This seems overwhelming at first, but when you marry it to your system, the only people that actually need to know all the checks are the QB and the Coach.   The players understand a few key terms, and that allows you to make adjustments quickly and in the middle of a game if needed. You can ONLY do this if you are putting in very few actual "plays". But as you can see, once the

concept is taught, you actually have multiple "plays".

One of the other great parts about teaching these **concepts** is that you can marry all these RPO tags with any run you put in. This allows you to take 3-4 run plays with 3-4 read looks, and now you have multiple different options off a very easy to learn offensive system. Getting maximum value for your practice time should be the goal of every offensive coordinator. After you have identified which **concepts** you will run, make sure your individual time matches up to these.

The entire goal of seeing the game as a basketball coach is that one **concept** becomes many plays as you and your players learn to adapt to what is being given to the offense. The offense also learns about how to accomplish their goal in multiple ways. Eventually you must become physical to run the ball, but this gives your line tools to have available for each scenario. This can be difficult for the coach, and sometimes the Quarterback, but once it is mastered it gives multiple options for you to choose from.

Concepts > Plays - Defensive Edition

"If you want team play, you must stress defense.   Defense makes players unselfish" – John Brady, Former Head Basketball Coach at Samford University, LSU, & Arkansas State

I began my coaching career in the great state of Alabama, and one thing I will say about that state is that they coach some great high school defenses. I've been blessed to be on a team that did not give up a touchdown for the first seven games of the season at Madison Academy. Nothing makes me more proud as a football coach than to see a great defense. We try to keep things as simple as possible for our players, but the goal is with 1-2 words we can give a different look to the offense to cause confusion.

Defensive football, like basketball, is about understanding simple **concepts** and reacting quickly. In this chapter, I will go through a few of the items that we use to help our players play faster. While I am a huge believer in simplifying, I don't believe in this because it is easier, I believe in this because it will allow us to have a great understanding of what we are doing. Most defensive coordinators (and I did this also) are very quick to continue to add in other stunts/blitzes before they are great at the **concept** they are teaching.

There are some awesome coverages and blitzes out there in the world of football. I watch and see them all the time and think about how we could use them. The same thing can be said of different coverages. What we do as a staff at the beginning of our season is consider the following questions when we look at base coverage and blitz concepts.

1) Can our athletes actually do this?

Having a realistic view of what your team, and the teams you will be competing with, is extremely important when you start to decide on any concepts you wish to teach. In the basketball world you see several styles that fit the athletes — from a press and run the floor team, to a grind the game and drain the clock team. In football you need to figure out what your athletes are going to have a chance to be successful with. Many times

> *Figure out what your athletes are going to have a chance to be successful with. The coach must adjust his scheme to match the talents of his players, not the other way around. Those who work in basketball are often more comfortable giving their athletes "cheats" to help them, but I have found in football we seem less willing to help our athlete. I do not understand this thinking.*

coaches use solid

schemes, but they don't match their athlete's ability. Be sure to put your players in the best position to be successful, even if that means having to work different aspects of the game you as a coach may not be as comfortable coaching. As a coach, I would much rather challenge myself and assistant coaches to have to learn techniques, than to put my athletes at a disadvantage due to their ability.

We have gone to a 3-4 cover 4 because we looked at the talent we had on our team and felt this would get our best players on the field with the best chance to win. We evaluated what the teams in our conference were doing — pretty much all spread — and felt this defense would give our athletes the best opportunity to win. If I could pick our defense, I was a huge 4-2-5 fan, but that didn't fit our personnel or what we needed to match up with in our conference. Be sure you pick what will benefit your athletes best, not simply "what you know". Each scheme has great points, but make sure it matches your players' ability level.

We want to also be sure to put players in an area where they can be successful with our scheme. The entire goal of an offense is to put defensive players in conflict, so we want to give them very simple rules so that they can attack and play fast. We understand that at times there are "holes" in every defense, but we want our guys to play fast and we teach them where the offense will attack us so that adjustments can be made quickly.

2) How long will this take to install and how long to master?

Once you have decided on an overall scheme, 3-4 or 4-3 or whatever you choose, figure out what your basic front and coverage will be. You will then need to think about how much time you will need to invest. I'd suggest 90% of your time needs to be on whatever is your "base". Become GREAT at what you will live in. I hear a lot of defensive coordinators talk about running very multiple stunts/coverages, but they are not good at any of them. We want to be GREAT at what we do and then start to build off it.

Be sure you marry your fronts and concepts to match your coverage. I've seen multiple teams that seem to struggle with this **concept**. If you want to bring pressure often and that is what you plan to do up front, you need to make sure you are playing tighter coverage (as the ball will come out quicker). If you plan to play more 3 to 4 man rush schemes against a QB, make sure you are putting your defensive backs in a position they can be successful — do not play man-to-man if you don't plan on pressuring the QB.

Find out which drills match what you hope to accomplish and make sure you are running these drills in individual time. If you are going to be a "reading front," be sure to teach your defensive linemen how to read blocks and spend most of your individual time teaching this. If you plan to stunt and move, be sure to work this in individual time. Try to decide what is the MOST important drill you could do, then move to the next drill and so on. Many times we want to "change it up" when running drills just to mix it up. I want our players to be GREAT at little things that make our defense works. This only happens if each position coach and defensive position understands how they fit in the defense.

3) **How many different ways can we run this — can we switch responsibilities easily and make one blitz/coverage look like 5?**

Of course great defenses do have the ability to mix up coverage and fronts to cause chaos with the opposing team. What our staff looks at is picking 1 (or at most 2) different blitz schemes that require bringing more than 2 blitzers. Once we have those schemes chosen to fit our personnel, we want to make sure all our players understand what we are trying to accomplish. After we have done this we simply teach each player that we can "switch" responsibilities, but it is the same **concept**. Therefore, we teach one blitz concept/coverage roll, but when we switch responsibilities it can look very different to an offense.

Here is an example of our "tango" blitz that most 3-4 teams have.

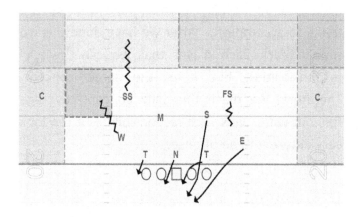

I don't want this to get into specifics of this blitz, but as a staff we do work hard to teach the general **concepts** we want to happen on any movement:

1) Late movement and disguise
2) Rules of blitzers - Aiming points and keys that can cause them to bend/break
3) Holes that will be created and need to be covered by other defenders

Once we have taught these concepts, we teach the actual "base" blitz. This one is a simple stunt off the edge with our Tackle working a 2-gap stunt attempting to draw the guard into the "A" gap.

Here it is when we call "Mango" — Switching responsibilities of the SAM and OLB

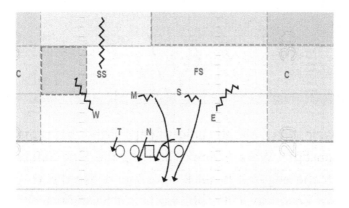

All we have done with this stunt is replaced our Outside Linebacker, but sending both our inside backers to an overload stunt. It is the same **concept**, but we like this one more against a balanced offensive set.

We can also run "Fango" — Switching the responsibilities of the FREE SAFETY and OLB.

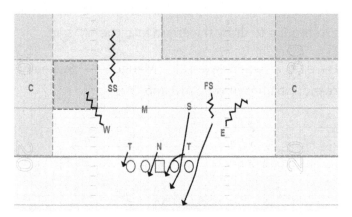

Again, very simple adjustment inside the same **concept**. We are simply bringing the Free Safety off the edge. It is quick adjustments like this that can be made if the offense is not accounting for him that will create a free rusher, without compromising the integrity of your blitz.

Once we have become very solid with this stunt, we can then begin to even play with it more. We also run "twist" on any tags with our DL/OLB if we want to switch responsibilities on blitzes. This allows us to have even more looks with our blitz packages that are much harder to pick up, but don't require much time. We work our "twist concept" during the offseason and we will hit it about 1-2 times a week early in the season. But our athletes understand what we are trying to do and they can go to it at any point. Often during the game,. they will ask for it because the offensive line is making calls and they understand it will get us a free player.

This would be an example of mixing "Fango" with a "twist" call so the Free Safety and the Mike would switch responsibilities

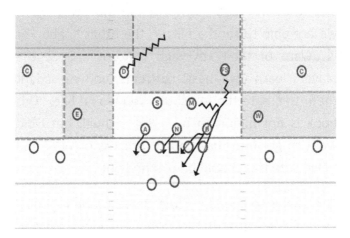

I don't know if we even called this exact stunt last season, but the **concept** holds and allows for your defense to be more multiple, but not more complicated. Using small tags, when all the players understand the **concept**, gives much more variety for the defense with very little time invested.

This can be done with really any blitz, and it gives

great freedom to a defensive coordinator. The options are as many as you want to work. We obviously don't spend a great amount of time working our free safety on blitzing, but we do in the offseason, and we review it to make sure he understands.

We also do the same concepts with coverage. We teach all the linebackers the coverage **concepts** and what we expect from them. That way when we are able to send a blitzer, the other linebacker is aware of their coverage **concept**. Once the players learn your basic **concepts**, you can adapt them to create the matchups you would like. This book is not meant to be a 3-4 manual, but I did want to get into the thought process of WHY and HOW defenses should be planned out.

The goal is to spend as little time putting in a blitz as possible, but get the maximum looks from it. We want to make sure our kids are very sound in what we do, so we don't do much. However, by teaching them all the **concepts** we can make very quick adjustments to all our blitzes and get a different outcome.

4) Can we run this against almost any front the offense may throw out at us with minimal adjustments?

When we pick blitzes or coverages, one of the first things our staff does is to see how this will look against most "normal" sets. While there are always outliers, we want to make sure our kids know what our "base" defense should look like against pretty much any offense we may see. We will obviously make game specific adjustments, but we want to know that if we get into a game and the offense runs something completely different from what we have seen, our athletes know how to line up and where their eyes should go.

We are overly simple with most of our blitzes and coverages, and often I wonder if it is too simple. The answer always seems to be that simple is the best for our athletes to know where to go and what to do very quickly. We love the 3-4 defense because of the easy adjustments, but any defense that is put in correctly will have the basic adjustments for each set. If you find yourself having to take a long time figuring out how to line up, more than likely you are making things too complicated. **If it is tough for the position coach**

to figure out, the athletes will never get it right. Be sure your athletes know what you are doing and also how it should be done.

Be sure that you have very simple to learn basic "rules", or as we have been calling them in this book **concepts** for your defensive players. We want our defense to be able to line up to any set that could possibly be thrown at us and know where their "keys" are and how they should attack the set. Here are a few basic examples that we give just one position on our defense to show what I am talking about.

> *Remember, hard for the coach is fine. Simple for the athlete is the goal.*

For the sake of teaching this I will choose one position group in our defense. Our Outside Linebackers have to move around often to make things work in our defense (as with most 3-4 defenses). We want them to have very simple alignment rules and very simple reads. Our read rules are as follows -

1) If the ball comes towards you -- play the outside hip of the ball carrier and attack.
2) If the ball goes away -- slow play and keep outside leverage.
3) If it is a pass -- follow your pass keys (and we only have 2 pass keys).

Because we have so few keys for our players, we are

able to work a ton of individual work to be very good at these keys. We work the different scenarios for our OLB if they are blitzing or if they are handling trips, etc...

By keeping their **concepts** very simple it enables us to work the scenarios they would see in games often. This allows us to be prepared for very quick in game adjustments (often times by the athlete on their own).

Again, this book is not meant to be a drill book of the 3-4 defense, but I want to point out that we try to give our athletes as few rules as possible, so that we can get as much time to work the **concept**. We have simple rules in their pass drops and simple rules for if they blitz. Our goal is that anything this position can do, there are very simple rules they can learn that will cover any situation they may find themselves in. This takes time for a defensive coordinator to learn, but for the athletes it is very simple.

Be sure to make ALL DRILLS work to help with these **concepts**. If you are running a drill that doesn't match, get rid of the drill. We want to spend time working players on drills that will directly help us on the field in a game situation. As a coach, that is where the great ones separate themselves. Running a very efficient and organized practice is key for growing in skills. If you cannot show me where this drill would happen on a Friday night, I don't want to see the drill run on Tuesday.

Back to our premise of thinking like a basketball coach, we want to have the flexibility to jump in and out of different looks in coverage and stunts, but keep all the players moving fast and not having to think... instead just play. This also will allow you as a defensive coach to match up better with offenses you will face from week to week, and even if you get a completely different look from a team than you had planned on seeing that night.

Adapt To Your Opponent

"The most dangerous phrase in our language is, 'We've always done it that way.'" - Admiral Grace Hopper

It amazes me week after week when we watch opponents' game film of how some teams have dominant athletes in space at slot WRs, and they have that player singled up against a linebacker. Or a team will have a very dominant running game and the opponents have a 5-man box. When you are coaching a team, I believe it is your job to give your athletes the best chance to win by taking away the opponent's best threats. I don't accept, "That's not something we do," from our defensive coaches. Our staff does a great job of making sure we do whatever is needed to make it difficult on the offense. Sometimes it is not enough to get the win, but we want to know we have always at least forced the team to beat us with other players on their roster, not their best player.

Bill Belichick said, *"I think it's relatively easy to game plan against a team that can only do one thing"*.

Belichick's New England Patriots are probably the best team in the NFL when it comes to defensive game plans. When you are watching your upcoming opponent, remember the goal is to beat them, so do whatever it takes to make that happen. That may require you to work a few adjustments to your defense. Nothing hurts me more than to hear coaches say, "We can't do that in our system". Find a new system.

Adapting to beat an opponent is not something that can only be done one time in a season. As a team, your players and assistant coaches must understand that each week requires tweaks due to an upcoming opponent. We often work these during the offseason/summer just to practice them in scrimmage scenarios. As a head coach I look ahead to our schedule for that season and know a general idea of what we will face so that we can begin preparing for situations we will see that season. I want to have as many tools available to me as possible. I have always attempted to have multiple different looks in our playbook and some concepts of how we can shift from one to the other with simple tags. The same is true on defense as we discussed in the earlier chapters. The goal is to go into the game with a grouping of blitzes and coverages as the main game plan, but always having the full play-sheet to work from if you need to make adjustments during a game.

Adapting to your opponent is often misunderstood by people that are staunch supporters of one of these two mindsets -

We are going to run what we run, and run it so well it doesn't matter what the other team does. We will focus on ourselves.

This mindset finds it hard to adapt, because coaches feel they are losing their identity, and they are not going to be as fundamentally sound at what they do. These teams tend to struggle when the opponent is evenly matched or has 1-2 superior athletes that they will not attempt to adjust to take away. Putting some poor defensive back in man-to-man coverage with no help against a D1 receiver is not a great recipe for success.

The same can apply to your offense. When we are facing a team with some great athletes, not only do I want our coaching staff to have some answers, but I want to make sure all our athletes are aware of what we are going to do, so we can be successful. We still run our offense, but we adapt to the situation of the game. Players need confidence, and I feel the best confidence is to acknowledge what the opponent may have an

While there is nothing wrong with having an identity, as a coach we must always have some tools to give our athletes when they may be physically out matched.

advantage in, but giving answers to our players of how we will still be successful.

We run a new offense each week with 50 new plays, and 7 coverages to take advantage of the opponent.

Most of the time this group tends to have no identity and is usually not great at anything they do. These teams struggle because they are generally not very good with simple fundamental skills. This is generally a younger coach that is very enthusiastic and has the best intentions of helping his athletes win. The problem with this is that the athletes cannot possibly retain all this information from week to week if there is no set system.

As a coach, I encourage our assistants to come up with several **concepts** during the weekend that we may want to look at for that game. But we generally come together as a staff and pick 1-2 that may mesh well with what we are already doing and we feel we can get coached up great that week.

We want to make sure that everything we do we have struggled with and argued over as a staff. The struggle is the learning process. If you are choosing something you will run as part of your system, it needs to be a **concept** you believe in and understand. When it is 4th and short, we want our players to understand what we will run and why we are running it. We don't want confusion in those critical moments or unbelief.

The key is to attempt to find a balance between the two of these types of thinking. Having a very fundamentally sound team that has an identity, but is willing to adapt to what the other team is giving them is the goal. Being able to work within your system with pre-set adjustments or very simple moves during a game have always seemed to work much better for our team. You must also be able to scout your opponent and find out what are the most important goals you wish to accomplish. The key to being able to adapt is to have such an understanding of your own **concepts** that these adjustments are something that should be very simple to make without compromising the identity of what your program is.

Scouting an opponent

1. The first thing I look for when scouting another team is not necessarily their best player, but which player touches the ball the most and why. Our number one goal is to do our best to either limit their touches or have more defenders at the point of attack to give us a chance to stop these players. While most offenses strive for balance, it is usually clear who the player is they want to go to in big situations. We feel if we can stop this player, or at least make it difficult on him, we can hurt the offense.

2. The next thing we look for on film is what I call the "average fan" game-plan. Find their guys that make you notice them if you were just a fan watching the game. Those are the studs. Sometimes we run all the reports and forget the most basic idea in football - stop the opposing team's players. Design your defensive game plan to make sure these guys have very limited opportunities to hurt you.

3. How are they using their best players — This includes linemen. Great coaches on the offensive side of the ball do a lot of subtle things to give their best athletes advantages. As a defense we want to make sure we are matching personnel with the

offense. For example - I've seen many times that a defense will adjust to cover the #3 WR with a linebacker or safety. This is also our adjustment most of the time. However, if the offense is moving their best player to that spot, we need to be sure to have adjustments made to get a better matchup, or help, on him. We also want to find out what the offensive line struggles with by position, and try to create matchup problems for them. If they have a weak side of the line, we may get our best Defensive Lineman on that side. If they have a very strong Lineman, we may try to put a faster athlete across from him. Just be sure you are matching personnel to hurt the offense as much as possible.

4. Who is the other team "hiding"? Find their weak links. I won't go into great detail here as the next chapter will cover this more in depth. As a staff, you need to find the best opportunities for your team to exploit.

5. Can the QB run and pass the ball? We need to figure out what he does best. Do we want to pressure him (that answer is pretty much 99% yes) or do we think that he is looking to run and we want him in the pocket? Find out what has given them problems, and be sure to implement that

into your game plan. With 80-90% of offenses in today's game, if you can fluster the quarterback you can really hurt the offense. The talent of the quarterback will dictate our how we roll coverage as well. I've worked with our defensive backs on aggression level if we feel we have a very predictable quarterback, and we usually do well with this. Jumping routes and reading eyes are something we game plan for on Monday after our coaching staff has judged the opposing quarterback.

After we answer all of those questions, then I am willing to start looking at the traditional breakdown of what formations the team runs and all the percentages of what they try to run from each. We do the same thing with the opponent's defense. I am not concerned with just numbers. I want to know WHY a team is doing what they are doing. That is why we attempt to answer the questions I listed first. After understanding the personnel of a team, the numbers from what they are running will allow you to create a much better game-plan.

> *I am not concerned with just numbers. I want to know WHY a team is doing what they are doing.*

Bill Russell said, *"Basketball is a game of habits. If you make the other guy deviate from his habits, you've got him."*

Basketball coaches in general do a very good job of setting their defense to stopping players and attempting to take what an offense does well out of the game. As football coaches, I feel we think it is much more difficult to be specific, since we have to be sound in our scheme. Great coaches and schemes teach the athletes **concepts** inside of their defensive scheme, and then make adjustments for what they will see each week. These should be thought about and implemented in the offseason and just brought in when needed each week. Having the ability to make quick changes makes teams great. Waiting until the half or next week to make adjustments will leave you with a lot of regrets.

As a team you must also look for people that you must attempt to avoid on defense. Sometimes it is not possible, if the player is a middle linebacker or is a nose tackle, but if it is possible you are doing a disservice to your players by giving that athlete the chance to wreck your game plan. Instead look for ways to formation them out of where you plan to attack. Or at the very least, figure a way to dedicate two players to them in the blocking scheme. Most of the time at the high school level, there are not 11 studs on defense, so decide who you want to attack and who not to attack.

This also applies to special teams. I would highly recommend not kicking the ball to the other team's best athlete if you have a kicker with that ability. Make them beat you with their players that are not as talented. Often, in special teams we have also intentionally not blocked players we had not seen make tackles and instead double teamed the best players on a team. Remember at all times that if a team can beat you with their lesser players, they were probably going to be able to beat you no matter the circumstance, but don't allow them to simply beat you playing the way they want to play.

I'd also highly recommend keeping a file on opposing coaches you face. At the high school level this is a little more difficult due to constant turnover, but having a knowledge of how the other guy thinks and what they like to do helps. Coaches will adapt, but we tend to always have many of the same tendencies.

My next goal is to begin keeping a file on officiating crews. I read recently that many college coaches have been working to know the penalty rate of each crew so they could prepare for how the game most likely would be officiated. We have already worked with our players about playing in specific stadiums and the issues we have faced (slick turf, loud band, etc). Adapting to your opponent is the main thought of this chapter, but we also attempt to have our players prepared for the environment they will be playing in.

Coaches must also make very quick adjustments in game. While each coach needs to have built in answers to potential problems, football, like basketball, is very unpredictable. My suggestion would be to have specific coaches assigned to look at every position and look for adjustments that may be needed. While it is ultimately the head coach that must make the call, having a staff trained to make quick adjustments is a huge asset.

Early in my career we would have our weekend meeting, and I'd hear from multiple younger assistant coaches about ideas they had, but were not sure if they should speak up. I now have a system (it must be organized) for coaches to speak and suggest. Often we will take the suggestion, but we have also had discussions about understanding that not all suggestions will be taken and to not take that personally. The goal is simply having a clear line of communication for ideas that can help us win.

Adapting too much can be a dangerous thing, but refusing to adapt is going to ensure that your program and team will have a low ceiling of success. Balance is the key, but the more I am around the game of football, the more I am impressed with watching established coaches in our profession recognize the young talent and adapting their systems to improve their programs. Continuing to look for ways to maximize your team's ability should be at the top of every team's wish-list, and it is very attainable for those willing to constantly adapt.

"Enjoying success requires the ability to adapt. Only by being open to change will you have a true opportunity to get the most from your talent." - Nolan Ryan

Attack A Person

"When you find your opponent's weak spot, hammer it". - John Heisman

Many times when I watch Coach Belichick's Patriots it is amazing that he can target whoever he feels is the weakness for the opponent and go right after them. It is almost like he is making his game-plan so painfully simple that you are sure the opponent will make adjustments. Often they do, and then he goes to the next part of his game-plan. As a Miami Dolphin fan I've been forced to watch him attack the worst player on the defense over and over. Simple and effective is the best way to set your game plan.

In the 2019 NBA playoff season I watched the Golden State Warriors come close to winning their 3rd straight championship and was interested to see what I felt great coaches were doing to attack them. The teams would put whoever Steph Curry (a great player, but apparently considered a sub-par defensive player) was guarding into a pick and roll. I won't go through all the basketball terminology since this book is geared for football coaches, but basically they were trying to get Curry to guard their best player by making him switch with the pick. Over and over again you'd see them get the matchup they wanted, and it usually worked in their favor. And basketball has only 5 players. Football has 11, so you know there is an 11th best player on the field. Go after him.

As football coaches, too often we get stuck into putting our players in specific positions and fail to get our best guy the best matchup. One season we played a team that was a typical man-to-man team that would match their cornerback to our outside wide receiver and their safeties on our inside wide receivers. They would isolate one of their linebackers on our back. We put in what I considered a simple "flip" call to put our running back at outside wide receiver, and our best player was now matched up on the guy we wanted. We ran verticals and simply called routes to our best player vs. their weakest cover guy. I'm not the smartest guy in the world, but I can call routes when my best player is matched up on the defender we want. This is why New England always has a running back that seems to have 80-90 catches a season. They get their athlete matched up in space against a defender that is not comfortable in coverage.

Simple formation movements or motions can accomplish this in the passing game. We do several things to get matchups that we like. Moving

Football is not played on a whiteboard. It is played with athletes, so just getting the right "numbers" does not guarantee that you will have success. I want the numbers and the athletes in my favor at all times on offense.

players around allows you to get your best player on other teams' worst player. It is so simple, yet not used enough. Most teams have pretty simple checks to formations or motion you may use. Run each formation early in the game, and you should have a good idea what look the offense will get. This will allow you to call plays based not only on alignment, but also personnel. Football is not played on a whiteboard. It is played with athletes, so just getting the right "numbers" does not guarantee that you will have success. I want the numbers and the athletes in my favor at all times on offense.

One of our motions we run now in our program is called "Patriot" where we bring our outside receiver into motion and now have him matched on a safety or can stack our receivers to get a free release. We call it "Patriot" because I watched the New England Patriots use this motion over and over to gain advantages in the passing game. By one very simple motion they accomplish 3 things:

1. Identify if the defense is in man to man or zone.
2. Gain a free release and create a natural bunch set.
3. By bringing a man farther in motion we can get the matchup on a linebacker

Here is an example of "Patriot" motion.

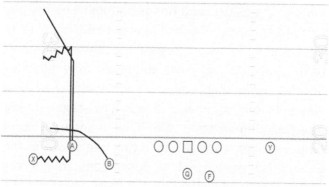

We run a few different **concepts** off of this motion, but here is a simple snag concept. The reason I show this is that many teams now do an excellent job of using formations and motions already built into their offense. Using these motions to gain the advantage is what I am after. I am not big on formations or motions just to do them. I want to use them only if we are gaining an advantage.

The simple goal is to get your best guy on their worst guy in the passing game. **Concepts** are wonderful and great against zone coverage. But even against zone coverage we want to get our best guy the ball (or we may need to reconsider what we are doing). In high school football it would be a huge luxury to have 4 weapons that are equal. Rarely have we had this. So we must be creative to get our best guys the majority of the targets.

Find a way to get your best guy free. Don't stick him at "x" position and not allow him to be the guy you are throwing the ball to most of the time. In my opinion, balance is something teams that don't have studs do. On the defensive side we love nothing more than when a team sticks their best player in one spot and leaves him stagnant. We now can double cover him if we want or bracket him. Essentially we can take that player out of the game. Use movement or formations to get the match-up you want!

Not to be overlooked, we also want to attack people in the run game. Scheme is important. Please do not misunderstand me, but we want to go with our best against their worst. As a coach, this will also require some time in the film room. You must identify who you want to attack in the running game and what they struggle with. The next part is getting into a formation that will get that defender lined up where they are most vulnerable. Finally, if possible, get them double teamed or trapped (whatever their weakness is) to gain maximum advantage.

Another way to get this done is to shift or motion (this seems to be a theme) your formation late if the defense has specific guys on their "weak side". If you identify a weakness, figure out how they line him up. Is the defense flopping to strength or field?

Once you have it identified, run at them. In one game we played, we ran "weak" 20 times because they didn't move that guy. One game we lined up and called the play away from a stud defensive end. This may sound overly simple, but why would a coach want to run into the teeth of the defense?

Even another way to accomplish this in the running game is to work on scheme adjustments as was discussed in the second chapter. Do not simply bang your head into the wall running a play that your offensive line can't block. Give them the tools. Football is not played on a whiteboard. Offensive has such a massive advantage, but often we don't take the advantage by simply going after the 1-2 favorable matchups you have. Often this is obvious in the skill positions, but I don't think many coaches take advantage in the running game by getting your guys the matchup they need upfront. We have moved offensive linemen around if possible to gain an even bigger advantage. The #1 goal on offense is to be able to move the ball and score points, and if your athletes understand the run game **concepts,** you should be able to make quick adjustments to gain an advantage.

Defensively, this is much more difficult, since you must work to hide deficiencies. However, it can be done with a little willingness to think outside the box. The goal of the game is to keep the opponent to as few points as possible, and the best way to do this is to eliminate their best players. Don't forget this simple point when you are working your defensive scheme. Often, as coaches we will over-think the process or simply rely on our base rules without putting any thought into stopping the best player(s) on the opposing team.

We also want to identify the weakest players on the opposing offense. Once this is done, we can do multiple things to help our game plan. Often we will blitz this player, or put our best athlete against him on the defensive front. If it is a skill player, we will blitz from them or roll coverage to force the ball into their hands. If a team is balanced, it is much more difficult, but even then we want to make the weakest link on the offense beat us. Often times a high school quarterback will still force the ball into
coverage attempting to get the ball to his best weapons, and now we can dedicate more people to them.

It seems so simple, but I've had to listen to many defensive guys saying, "We can't do that," or "We run our system". My system is to take away your best player, period!

Back to our basketball example, we used to tell several of our defenders to leave non-skilled players open to encourage them to shoot the ball. This is something that is done very often in basketball. Sometimes it is a guy that can't go left and you force him to beat you playing how he doesn't want to play. The best example of this is Bill Belichick and his defensive theory. They force teams to beat them with their worst players, and their #1 goal is to take away your best player. If you beat me with your third or fourth option, then I will accept it and not lose any sleep after the game. But if I am getting beat over and over by your best guy, we are going to do everything within our power to stop him.

We have played multiple teams in my tenure as head coach that took who we viewed as their best threat and played him at receiver. We will make sure he doesn't see single coverage at all, or at least very rarely. As a coaching staff we are honest with our players that we feel the other players are solid, but "X" player is the guy we want to be sure to dedicate our defense to stopping. We can work several **concepts** during that week in practice, but a good offensive coordinator will always have something up his sleeve. If our athletes know why we are doing what we are doing, many times they will make the in game adjustments with very little help from us. Be sure your athletes understand why you are doing what you are doing on defense and often they will make plays that make a coach look smart!

To be able to attack the other team, you must do quite a bit of film study and scouting. It doesn't take much to turn on the tape and figure out who the best players are. When we are breaking down an opponent I do want to know that, but I also ask our staff for the following:

1. **What is this player's best skill?**

    Once you have figured out what the opponent does well, then pass on the information to your players. Often times I delegate most of this to my position coaches as they will be working with the players that must understand their opposition. We want to make sure our players respect (not fear) the player(s) they will be going against. By doing this we can give our athletes a realistic chance to at MINIMUM stop what the other player does best.

2. **How technical is this player?**

    Often times when our staff watches film we can figure out how the other players operate. If we can figure out how they are being coached and where their eyes go, we can give them several "false" keys. Some of these are built in our scheme, but many of these are small things we will teach the individual player to take what the opponent is doing and use it against them. When you understand how the other player is coached and will react, you can take advantage.

If the entire team is very technical, then we will work in 2-3 small wrinkles (usually already installed in the spring/summer) with our team that will attack the other team. Offensively, this may be a tagged route that we have not shown on film, or it may be using the defensive linemen's technique against them. Defensively, this may be a specific blitz or working our defensive backs to keying the eyes of the quarterback.

3.   What does this player struggle with the most?

Once we have figured out what the player struggles with the most, we will begin to game plan as a staff to attack this. We will also work with our players on how we can execute taking advantage of a player. ***I will note that this is not a session where we make fun of or belittle an opponent. Instead we show what they do well and what they struggle with**. I'd also recommend coaching up your scout team player that will be representing this player during the week. Many times we spend Sunday evening figuring out who on our team would be the best representation of the opponent. At times it has been a young assistant coach.

4. How do they handle adversity?

This can apply to any position, but we specifically look at guys that will have the ball in their hands often. We want to see how these players handle it when they are frustrated. Obviously you want to decide how to attack a quarterback, but we also look to how skill players handle it when things aren't going well for them. Will they become a cancer to their team and stop playing hard? If we find this to be the case, you can bet we will make sure this happens as much as we can accomplish it.

5.   **Can we cause them to turn the ball over**?

This one is pretty simple, but we want to chart the amount of times a team (or specific player) has turned the ball over, or put the ball in danger, which means a jump ball or ball on the ground. We work turnover drill each week, but on weeks that we have noticed this more, we will run these drills more often and will even work this much more in group time and team. While we always stress turnovers, on weeks we have noticed the ability to create more, we will be sure to coach our players where and when we expect opportunities to happen.

Whatever you decide to do, be sure you understand that during a game it is always best to give your team as many tools as possible to be successful. Ultimately, you are playing the opponent. I'll leave this idea with the following quote:

"The pessimist complains about the wind, the optimist expects it to change, but the realist adjusts the sails". - William Arthur Ward

Fundamentals Are King

"Basketball, like all sports, is predicated on the execution of fundamentals. The coach is a teacher. His subject -- Fundamentals." - Dr. Jack Ramsey

One of the greatest compliments I can get from an opposing coach is that my team played hard and played with great technique. We want to always give our team a chance to win by understanding the rules of the game and playing with great technique. It is hard as a coach to have the patience required to coach the small details and not move on to a much more "interesting" point in the offense/defensive scheme. I struggle with this every season as I want to put more stuff in, but the years I've been the most successful, I have instead focused on being very good at the simple parts of football.

When I became a Defensive Coordinator at the age of 25, I spoke with several of my mentors and they all said basically the same thing, "Don't worry as much about scheme. Teach them to tackle and line up right". Fundamentals are often overlooked in the game of football much more than you would

When we turn on film of teams, we notice very quickly the teams that are technically sound and become very concerned about how we will take advantage of them. Teams that are very good at fundamentals are very hard to beat.

see in other sports, specifically basketball. When we turn on film of teams, we notice very quickly the teams that are technically sound and become very concerned about how we will take advantage of them. Teams that are very good at fundamentals are very hard to beat. This past season our team won the conference title and we did it because our team understood how to do very simple things very well.

Jim Rohn said, *"Success is neither magical nor mysterious. Success is the natural consequence of consistently **applying** the basic fundamentals."*

The key word is **applying**. Too many times I watch coaches run drills, and they think that takes care of the fundamental skill set. This is NOT the case. Any coach has fundamental drills they run pretty much every day. We teach each position specific drills, and we work them often. Fundamentals are the key to being a great football team. However, just because you work a drill does not mean it will help you win. If the athlete cannot take that drill and apply it to an actual game situation, you are wasting your time.

What great coaches do

Make sure your athletes understand why they are working a drill. What is the primary objective of the drill and how does it help us be successful in a game. If they don't know, you might as well not even run the drill. Drills that cannot translate into a game are worthless. Make sure your athletes know how you value their time and that everything you do on the field is for a purpose.

Teach your position coaches the value of every drill you want them to run. Most assistant coaches want to be great at what they do, but many times

As a head coach I am constantly trying to find ways to cut down on practice time and increase time in the film room or weight room. To this end we make sure any drills we are going to run are worth the time invested. Fundamentals are king in all sports, but fundamentals are not simply drills to run drills. Have a plan and a purpose with how you advance from individual time to group time and from group time to team periods. The athletes and assistant coaches need to see how all of this we make assumptions they will run a drill how we want it run, or they even understand the importance of the drill. Make sure they know the objective and importance. What are the coaching points of this drill, how do we adjust the drill to fit the skill level of our athletes, and how do we modify this to fit in our scheme?

We have come up with a drill book each off-season. I stress to all my assistants that I want them to research some drills and see if they can help us. Then we go through and decide on what will and won't work. I want them to be creative and come up with something that will be useful for game situations. Be willing to think outside the box, but don't reinvent the wheel either. Take all the available resources and make them fit your scheme. When coaches have to work to come up with the drills they want to run, you know they will place much more value on them than simply seeing them on a practice schedule and a head coach teaching the basics of the drill.

Encourage your assistants to come up with new flavors of drills that apply to that week. I love seeing young assistants come up with their own drill that they can explain to me and our athletes how it will apply to this game. The athletes love something "new" and the assistant coach has taken ownership in his position group. As a head coach, you are only as effective as your position coaches when it comes to fundamentals.

Michael Jordan said, *"The minute you get away from fundamentals - whether it'/s proper technique, work ethic or mental preparation - the bottom can fall out of your game, your schoolwork, your job or whatever you're doing"*.

Be sure to not only teach drills and skills, but also make effort a fundamental key to success. Make film study something that is expected. Fundamentals are much more than running some kind of drill.

What do you prioritize in Fundamentals?
While as coaches we would like to be great at everything, there are only so many hours available to practice. We spend most of our time on fundamentals, but even with that being the case a coach must prioritize what he wants to spend most of his time on. Be sure that you know what is most important to you, and plan your practice time, film time and meeting time on these items. Football is a pretty simple game, but the best teams understand how each drill translates to the field -- if drills don't show up on Friday, stop running them.

This book is not meant to go through drills and plays. Instead it is to give a general overview. With that being said, each coach must pick what they feel is most important, but here is the list of general qualities that I require our assistant coaches to value:

Offensively

1. Unselfishness:

The main idea we preach to our offense is the willingness to block for each other and to not be concerned with who runs the ball, or catches the ball. We want our players to work hard for each other. To make this happen, we usually start our spring practices and early summer practices with a blocking circuit for each position. The quarterbacks will work selling the fakes during this period. We want each player to know that for us to be successful, our players must sacrifice for each other.

One of the unique things we do, that we didn't do on purpose at first, is give all our younger quarterbacks another position. We used to do this out of need, but have since figured out that a quarterback that has earned his stripes playing another position has a few things going for him:

1. The other players know he is willing to play away from the ball.

2. He has learned that it takes an entire team for him to have success.
3. Knowledge of the game is increased.

2. **Physical play:**

Football is different than basketball in many ways, but the most glaring difference is the level of physicality that it takes to play football. There are plenty of drills available, but we want to make sure our team understands that we expect them to play more physical than any opponent we will play. We teach this throughout the spring/summer/off-season in the weight room, and we continue this onto the field. While we are careful not to go to the ground very often, we do not want to turn into a 7-on-7 team that does not value physical play.

Being physical is a mindset we want to instill in our players from the start of spring. We want them to understand that at times they will simply need to want it more than the opponent. This gets into the mental part of the game, which I will cover later in this chapter.

3. **Ball Security:**

The first statistic I would want to know if I was to predict a win or loss from any football team would be the turnover ratio. I am sure each team places a premium on this aspect, but we want to be sure our players understand that there are times we are ok with our players being much more aggressive with the football. I believe when our players understand the situations in the game and that we feel we will win the game if we win the turnover battle, they understand the importance of taking care of the ball.

Be sure to teach the details of ball security as well. Understanding at times "when the ride is over" and going down to protect themselves and the football is an important skill to teach ball carriers. We also talk about the only times we ever want the ball being put away from our body would be on 4th down --

NEVER reach for the pylon unless it is 4th down.

4. **Penalty free:**

The other issue that has hurt many offenses, including ours, is drive killing penalties. While we have not mastered that concept by a long way, we are working daily on what we expect from our team. Nothing will drive a coach crazier than a false-start, or a holding penalty away or behind the play. If I could pick one area that when we do well in our offense functions well, this would be it. We also focus by position group on teaching blocking without holding.

5. **Effort:**

I included this in fundamentals on offense and defense. I do think this can, and must, be coached. It may take a while, but this can become part of your culture. As was mentioned earlier in the book, work to motivate your team through different ways. I have found that most players want to work hard, but they just don't know how to do it. Coach your "stars" even harder on effort. Most of the time a few film sessions will do the trick. Do not assume that it is going to be a different level than what you are seeing in practice. What you get on Tuesday is typically what you see on Friday.

Defensively

1. Tackling:

This should go without even needing to be said, but tackling in football is the most important skill that must be taught to a defensive player. If you are very good at teaching these skills your defense will improve more than any scheme you may put in. There are very good drills to work on with tackling and even complete books written about this skill because it is the most important part of defense. One thing I would encourage is to work position specific tackling drills as you get into the season. Your defensive linemen need to work different tackling drills than your defensive backs. Make

Do not assume that it is going to be a different level than what you are seeing in practice. What you get on Tuesday is typically what you see on Friday.

sure the type of tackling drills you are running apply to what a player will see during a game. Scheme is important, but ultimately we want our players to be the best they can possibly be at tackling.

2.   **Communication:**

After tackling, we feel this is the most under-coached part of a great defense. It is not natural for many players and is needed on every team. There are not very many specific drills we run in this area, but we make sure it is constantly used in each period we run. It is very difficult for some coaches that tend to be very detail oriented (myself) to step back and allow the defenders to not communicate during practice, but you must allow them to see how bad it will go if they are not constantly communicating. The last thing we want to hear being said on the sideline after a blown assignment was, "I thought". Over-communicate from head coach to assistant coach, from assistant coach to player and from player to player.

One thing I make sure my players understand is that just because "I said it" doesn't mean it was communicated. Players on the field must make sure everyone knows what is going on each play. Repeating and forcing them to talk is something we start on day 1. The best way to enforce this is to stop practice right before a snap and ask a random player what we are in on defense and how he knows. After we run a few gassers for not communicating, our players figure out pretty quickly that they must get it right before the snap.

We also work very hard to make sure our defensive backs are constantly talking during any pass concept if we are in zone. We want to make sure they are all on the same page at all times. I've often said the old coaching adage, "If we are all wrong, then we are all right". As long as we are talking it may not be the perfect "fundamental" way to run a coverage or stunt, but when we understand that the **concept** is to cover each receiver, we are fine with them switching or not as long as they both do the same thing. There will be plays that are very tough to defend and we want to make sure we are constantly communicating.

3.   **Alignment:**

After coaching for several years, we wanted to work hard to eliminate all what we considered simple fixes. Alignment on defense was an area that we never wanted to come back to as a staff and find guys out of position. This sounds very simple, but we are talking more than just about base alignment in the middle of the field on 1st and 10. As a staff we wanted to make sure our players knew the adjustments with field position, down and distance and blitz/coverage changes. This even goes into how we want to blitz -- start from width and depth and attack in the straightest path possible to the targeted area. It all begins with alignment on defense.

This goes not only to alignment, but also stance. Teaching the minor details to each athlete from foot position to hand placement is important (on both sides of the ball). However, even more important is that the athletes understand WHY they are doing what they are doing. When an athlete understands that football is a game of inches and you can show them that, they are going to become eager to learn the nuances in minor details.

4.   **Keys/Angles:**

Another big fundamental for us on defense is where we want our players' eyes going. Where they look is where they will move, so we work very hard to train the eyes of our defenders. We also work very hard to work on our fits. Most of the teams I have coached need to play faster than they run a 40-time. Many players will become very good if they can focus on a simple key. It shrinks the game and makes their job easier. While they must understand the grand scheme of what is going on, they must also be able to react quickly, and that can be done by giving them a very easy to read key. In our defense we want that key to be correct over 90% of the time and often spend the entire weekend finding the key that makes our players correct.

We can do this if we teach angles and fits correctly. There are some pretty simple drills we run to work our player's angles -- **I am not a fan of running to cones so everything we do is with moving parts and a live ball carrier. We will also force our players to point at their keys on Mondays after we put in our game-plan and again on Thursday practice. The players do not like this, but it forces them to narrow their focus and slow the game down.

5.   **Effort:**

Just like on offense we expect maximum effort from our players. We designate a few backside players that we teach to slow play, but we expect to have 9-10 helmets flying to the football at all times. Effort is something that can be taught, but the best way to teach it is to find ways to have your players hold themselves accountable. You also need high energy coaches that coach with great effort, and you as the head coach must show great effort if you are expecting it from your team.

I'd also highly encourage you to have your assistants come up with what fundamental skills they feel their position needs the most and rank them. Look at what list they come up with and make sure you are putting the right amount of emphasis on this in practice time and film time. Any way you can get coaches and players thinking about what they value most and placing an emphasis on it is a great thing. Make sure your drills match up with what your values are as a head coach.

Mental Fundamentals

"No building is better than it's structural foundation, and no man is better than his mental foundation". John Wooden

Be sure to train you athletes to be not just students of the game, but strong mentally. Mental ability can be improved on by athletes. Some are obviously much better in this area, but all can improve with great coaches pushing them. Having athletes that are great at technique is great, but having mentally tough kids is much more important. Be sure to incorporate this in your practices and off-season as much as you do drill work.

As a young coach, I fell in love with talent and would do my best to "look the other way" on a very talented player. When a coach does this I can almost predict the following will happen -- you will win the games you should win and winning does seem to cure a lot of issues, but the minute things get tough in a big game that athlete will crumble. If you are not pushing your athletes mentally, you are setting them up for failure. You are doing that athlete a disservice also because he needs to be coached up to his potential. Now, I am harder on my more naturally gifted athletes. I meet with each player that will play a big role and let them know that I will be much tougher on them than others because they have great ability, and I want to see them reach their full potential.

We try to set up 2-3 mental or effort drills during the off-season that we will rotate through. This is not simply running. We want it to be something that an athlete must engage their mind in during a tense situation. Explain to all your athletes what you are trying to accomplish, and actually hold their feet to the fire during these drills. We want to stress that these drills are not punishment, but they are testing their mental toughness.

Here are a few very simple ideas we have used to help challenge our kids' mental toughness:

1. Weight room drills

We attempt to focus on building better physical athletes through our off-season and in-season sessions in the weight room as a priority. But we have also attempted to find drills that can serve as a 2-for-1 in working mental toughness. We want to challenge athletes to compete and to work through pressure. If we can find any drill that is already working to improve speed/strength, and will not put the athlete at risk of injury (we would not want to do this with max effort lifts), we want to have athletes compete at all times.

I'm also a big fan of simple body weight exercises that do not take away from what we are trying to accomplish in the weight program. These exercises will burn the athlete's muscles, but they will recover almost instantly. Examples would be - Frozen pushups, Core Bridges, Wall sits, etc... This challenges the athlete mentally and forces them to be uncomfortable and push their limits. We attempt to do these types of challenges in two ways: 1) Competition among athletes and 2) Team working against the clock. Both are very effective in different ways.

2. Working team concepts into conditioning

There are times to simply line up and run. We try to limit these times to the month or two before our season starts. While there is no fundamental skill set being developed through conditioning, we are able to push our athletes. I am sure each program has their own flavor of conditioning. One of the ideas we started to push into our conditioning was to have special teams, defensive situations and offensive plays on air thrown in during the middle of conditioning. We want to see which athletes can function when they are exhausted physically.

3. Pressure plays

There is nothing more pressure packed in basketball than "pressure free throws." Pressure free throws are when an athlete takes the free throw with the team knowing that if they miss, everyone on the team runs. As a football coach, I wanted to find ways to create the same pressure on athletes that are going to have to produce with pressure in a game. We have now added in pressure field goals, pressure pass plays (must be into the endzone), pressure blitz packages and pressure special teams (punt must be downed inside the 20). This creates at least a similar pressure to these athletes to perform for the team.

Mental toughness can be improved upon. As a coach, how you deal with mental toughness will show up on game day. If you are not teaching it, you just get what hand you are dealt. If you can identify it early and work with your athletes, you may be able to improve them. We also want to know which players perform better with extreme pressure placed on them and which ones need to be calm throughout the game. Do not give up on a player that struggles with this, but work with them to help them recognize it and improve.

I'm a huge believer in speaking things into existence. I don't lie to my team, but I will work hard to point out the good in mental toughness or unselfishness. I'm a big believer that the team that is mentally tougher will perform significantly above what their "ability level" would suggest. Stress these to your team with positivity and often your athletes will rise to the occasion. Punishment is needed at times, but often praise gets the job done much more effectively. Many young athletes struggle with confidence and will only improve with experience and mentoring -not yelling and blaming.

David Hourne - *"Our behavior as an athlete is often determined by our previous experiences and how we dealt with those experiences. It is these experiences from past performances that can often shape what will happen in the future. It is for this reason that you learn and move on to be more mentally strong as both an athlete and as a human!"*.

There are many books that only discuss the mental part of athletics for a very good reason. This part of the game is often neglected by many coaches, since it is very hard to measure. As a head coach, I try to come up with a list of items we can tie to mental toughness:

1. Red zone efficiency on offense and defense

While some may think this is not in the "mental" part of the game, there are specific parts that we work on often with our players. While we may give up a score in the red zone, or not perform well on offense, there are a few specific areas that we attribute to the mental part of the game:

-Understanding how to use the field to your advantage on defense

-Jumping routes or Jumping the snap to gain an advantage

-Mentally staying engaged when momentum switches

-Never taking a sack on 4th down or holding on to the ball short of the goal line (we teach fumbling into the endzone on 4th down or 2-pt plays).

2. Third/Fourth efficiency on offense and defense

This is very similar to red zone efficiency. We want to make sure our players are always aware of the situation in the game. As coaches we want to make sure we are doing the following items:

-Routes on offense are past the 1st down if designed that way.

-Coverage always is dictated by the sticks.

-Understanding and playing the game with the knowledge of the very big difference between 3rd and 4th down

-Never committing pass interference short of the first down

3. "Bad turnovers" and turnovers we "cause"

While all turnovers are bad, they are not all equal. We do not consider turnovers (especially interceptions) as bad on 3rd and long or 4th down. There are also some turnovers that are much worse, like those committed on 1st down or unforced fumbles. While we prize ball security like any team, we really want to focus on what we are able to control offensively.

On the other side of the ball, we take great pride in "causing" turnovers. In some games the defense simply benefits from the offense making mistakes, but great defenses actually cause turnovers. Most interceptions or "caused" turnovers and fumbles that we strip, we count in this category also. In my opinion most turnovers that are forced are due to mental preparation coming to fruition on the field. A defensive player must have been working above simply tackling or attempting to survive to cause a turnover. **We also consider recovered onside kicks as turnovers we have caused and put a huge emphasis on this area.

4. Pre-snap penalties

This one is pretty self-explanatory, but any pre-snap penalties are unacceptable. Going one step farther are what we would consider terrible pre-snap penalties. Being offside on 3rd down, especially if it results in a first down, is one of the worst penalties a defense can commit. We also include alignment penalties on the offense as worse than jumping the snap. Any pre-snap penalty is not a good thing, but some we recognize as worse than others. We also teach when we are ok with a pre-snap penalty - goal line defense we may intentionally try to time up a snap to make a play.

5. Post-snap penalties

After the play, penalties are another form of mental weakness in athletes. Almost every time these penalties are completely unnecessary and will quickly land one of our players next to a very upset coach. We do not consider facemask or borderline late hit calls in this category. While we don't want these penalties to happen often, they are simply lack of technique or bad luck.

When an athlete commits a penalty after the play that they can control, they are telling the team by their actions, that they do not care about winning, they care about their own ego. This is a sign of mental weakness and is something that must be instantly fixed. I have found that while a harsh punishment is due, there needs to also be a deep conversation with the athlete to help them understand why these penalties must stop.

6. Missed assignments

While missed assignments can happen from time to time, almost every time they are due to lack of focus. There will be times that an athlete may see something for the first time in their career and will make a mistake (or blown assignment), but most of the time these happen due to lack of focus or lack of awareness by athletes.

7. Loafs

Most coaches understand this category so I will not say much. However, in my experience, I have noticed that we don't seem to have nearly the amount of loafs or "minor injuries" when we are winning. It takes mental toughness to be able to continue to play with great effort when the game is not going how a team wanted it to go.

We want to condition our athlete's mental toughness to be able to respond when things don't go well on the field. While we have tried many different incentive programs with mental toughness, the best way to help it exist is to continue to teach these situations during the off-season and during practices. This does not always mean punishment when the athletes fail, but it can. We want to make sure we are teaching as much as possible and that our athletes understand why all these areas are important. We use punishment from time to time, but often simply teaching your athletes how these areas will help them be successful will be enough.

> *We preach to our team that we may get beat by a great play or great talent, but never allow ourselves to get beat by our own mistake.*

What Fundamentals are not

1. **Drills run that we have seen other teams run**

Don't start running a drill "because team X is running this drill", or "I saw this college run the drill". Find out what makes this drill effective. All drills are not equal and all drills may not apply to your athletes. Be sure to have done research on the coaching points and application of any drill before you start to run it with your team. I am one of the world's biggest proponents of taking great drills and learning what makes them great, so I am not saying don't use what another coach has come up with and evolving it to fit your program. The main point is to be sure you understand WHY you are running a drill, not simply running something you have seen some other coach/program run.

2. **Skills that do not translate into what we want to accomplish**

Ask your players if they can tell you when you would use this drill in a game. If they cannot answer or hesitate in answering, you need to either eliminate the drill, or do a MUCH better job explaining how it translates. Practice planning should take time and effort for each position coach. Too many times I watch coaches either run too many drills that are ineffective or only run drills they've run for many years, but haven't explained the importance to their players. Be sure to communicate why you are working any drill or skill set and how it will help you win games.

3. Running kids till they puke to make them "mentally tough"

While I do think athletes must be pushed mentally, and some of that does involve being in condition physically, which means they must be run, too often I see coaches running athletes into the ground with no real purpose other than, "to get them in shape". I am an advocate of getting athletes into shape, and honestly there is a time and a place to run sprints for football players. I've tried many different ideas (and some have not worked) to make conditioning apply to the game of football. It pains me to watch a lineman that will never move more than 20-yards at a time running gassers. We try to involve sled push, hill running, chute work or something that applies to those athletes. Just like I don't work my shot put/discus athletes in track the same as I do my 3200-meter runner, we want to make conditioning something that can apply to the team.

Fundamentals will always be the most important skill you can teach your athletes that is specific to their position. As a coach, you must decide what is the most important fundamental each position must understand, and once you have decided on them, be sure to make your practices match them. A team that is not only great at understanding the game, but also mentally strong can "overachieve" every season. *Mike Tyson said, "everyone has a plan until they get punched in the mouth".*

Understand The Why

"He who has a why can endure any how." - German philosopher Frederick Nietzsche

Great coaches are able to motivate many different types of athletes. I've told my assistant coaches on more than one occasion that the number one thing we must learn as coaches is how to reach different personalities. The main way this is accomplished is when everyone from coaches to players understand WHY our program exists. Not everyone you coach will want to be coached the same way, but most of them want to reach for their best. They just don't respond to the same type of coaching.

I once had to have a hard conversation with an assistant coach who was telling me he "couldn't coach player X" because he was hard to work with. My response was that it is easier for me to find a good position coach than a player that had his ability. Understand that this player was not a cancer or doing anything morally wrong. He was just not as easy to work with as many of our other players. While I supported the coach and helped with discipline for the player, we need to understand that not all players will respond to the same coaching style. I believe in treating players with an equal standard, but that does not mean treating them all the same. Find what works for each player, and use that to motivate them. The best coaches are able to understand why an athlete responds and find new ways to push them to perform at a high level.

In my experience, athletes and coaches will give you great effort and dedication if they understand why they are working for the coach. Yes, I believe they work for their head coach. You will have 10-15% of athletes that are going to be special character athletes and would work no matter what, but the majority of athletes/coaches work for the leadership. That is why it is often shared on social media that "people don't quit jobs, they quit bosses". In any program you will always have athletes that don't make it, but the great programs get the majority of their athletes to buy in and stay the course.

> *In my experience, athletes and coaches will give you great effort and dedication if they understand why they are working for the coach.*

The concept of your WHY is something you will have to decide on your own. Teams that are successful have a very clear goal and they understand what is expected of them. More importantly they also understand WHY this is the goal. You must be sure your athletes understand why they are playing for you as a coach. What do you stand for? What are the goals of your program? More specifically what are the goals for EACH of your players? Again, this is up to each individual coach, but whatever you decide it needs to be very clearly explained to your team.

Love for your players must be at the top of the reasons why you coach. I have been around a lot of really great coaches that were very different philosophically from offense to defense to how to run a practice, but each great one loved the kids. The coaches I have been around that I felt were not as strong or even weaker ones seemed to have lost or never really had a love for the players they coached. Most coaches care about their players, but you just have to care about them more than you do yourself. This sounds simple, but it is often the key to why some coaches burn out of our profession and some coach for 40 or more years. If you care for your players on a deep level, it will give you energy as a coach that many don't even know they have. 80+ hour work weeks are not hard when you understand your WHY as a coach.

What do you stand for as a program?
This concept is gaining ground now in almost all sports' programs and good businesses across the country. Anyone that wants people to work hard in their company, or any coach that expects maximum effort from his players, must understand what they want their company/team to be known for. I cannot give you a simple golden rule, or rules, that will work for you and your program because they must be something you believe in

and struggle to come up with as a coach. But I can give you some ideas of what our program stands for:

1. **Doing whatever we can to keep young men in our program** so we can teach them how to become better young men of character. We give 2nd and 3rd chances as long as a player is willing to work with us and accept their punishment. I cannot reach young men if my first instinct is to kick them off the team. Talent is not going to factor into this decision, but if I feel we can help this young man without risking losing others, we will always try to work with them. As a side note, if you decide to adopt this in your program, you must understand that this is not the easy route. This will require working with some athletes that are difficult to work with and who will be a constant headache for the coaching staff. I have put some athletes off the team, or had several decide they don't want to face the punishment that would be given and they quit, but my goal has always been to give as many opportunities as I can without putting other athletes on our team at risk.

   I always think of my own children when I am coaching these young men. I've had times that my wife has had to help me remain calm with how angry I was with their behavior, but not one time have I ever even considered kicking them out of my house. I do whatever I can do to fix the behavior and teach them. Discipline is helping young men improve, not cursing or shouting.

Understand that I am in no way suggesting sacrificing a high standard. Actually the opposite. I tell my players that because I care for them I will not allow them to be less than the best they can become. And at times discipline does require punishment, but more importantly it involves teaching and patience.

2. **Expecting maximum effort at all times from players/coaches**. No coaching with your hands in your pockets or being low energy with your players. Work hard and your players will follow. You could write an entire book on this principle, but we prioritize effort over almost any other attribute. I hire coaches and pick who will play, all based off this principle. I don't always pick the smartest or most talented. I want the guys that will give maximum effort at all times. It is much easier to teach the game of football to someone than to teach them how to give great effort.

I always assumed this would not be an issue with assistant coaches, but I learned quickly that just like players, they must be mentored and shown what is expected. I attempt to show this by example as I feel the leader should always be the hardest worker. Another way to teach assistant coaches is to let them know the importance of what we are doing for these young men on and off the field. If those tactics do not work, then you may have to resort to something more drastic, but I've always tried to work in a positive manner first.

3. **Encourage before you criticize** -- I want our program to be a place people want to come every day to work hard. This does not mean we don't coach our players or discipline them, but it means we want this environment to be encouraging. I want my criticism to be heard, and if I am constantly doing it, it is tuned out. I also teach my players that it is my job to be the guy that nobody likes. Their job is to lift up their teammates. I give my assistant coaches the same excuse as well -- always blame me when they are tough on a player.

I was taught as a young teacher and coach to work with the "sandwich method" when dealing with criticism. Start with something positive and try to end with something positive. In the middle (or the meat of the conversation) is where you give your critique and hand out any punishment that may be needed. Working in that manner hasn't solved every issue I have dealt with, but it has helped diffuse many situations.

4. **Everyone has value off the field** -- The reason I became a coach was to help young people grow. Often as a coach, we lose our focus and priority due to many of the constant distractions or pressure from parents or administration or our own

personal goals. I want each of my players to know I care for them. YOU CANNOT FAKE THIS. It must be real and it must be at the top of your priority list. This also needs to extend beyond players -- it should encompass assistant coaches, managers, and volunteers in your program as well. Being genuine with your care for those around you is not going to guarantee you win on the scoreboard, but it will guarantee you win in life.

Being genuine is the most underappreciated quality that separates leaders that have the respect of others from those that must lead through fear or some other means. I have tried to emulate several coaches that all have different abilities, but the one quality they all share is that they are genuine people. Athletes respond to coaches they recognize are not putting on a show, but simply being who they are.

What are your goals for EACH player?
I have found that very successful coaches make sure each player understands their role on the team. This doesn't have to be an overly-negative or false conversation. I've always felt each player on the team that has given effort every day deserves to know what you expect from them. Be honest in these conversations, and I'd recommend having at least one other coach (preferably their position coach) in the room for the conversation. If nothing else, we want our athletes to at least know going into a season (or even a specific week, if their role has changed) what to expect.

We want our players that will not see the field to understand our value of them as a person. We also want to explain to them how they can help the team even if it may not be in the role they wish they had. Surprisingly to me, these conversations usually go pretty well. Players want to know that you care about them, and you are aware of the sacrifice they are putting in each day. Most of these players are aware that for one reason or another, they will not get to play much on Friday night, but we want them to understand what their expectations are.

As important, is the conversation with your "stars" of the team. They need to understand that you will push them and be harder on them than anyone else on the team. Most of them will accept it if they understand WHY you are doing this.

Luke 12:48 says it well "*...from everyone who has been given much, much will be demanded*". Push your stars, but be sure they understand WHY you are on them so much. My goal is to grade them at what their ability would suggest they attain. I am very honest with them and don't play mind games about if they will play, since most can see what is very clear, but we do explain that we expect more from them. We also explain that their number one job is to make sure nobody else on the team will say they are outworking them.

When you as a Coach understand your WHY and your team understands it and believes in it, there are not many limits to what your program can achieve. I cannot choose your WHY, but it must be something that each program understands. If you do not set a goal and a standard, your players and assistant coaches will never be able to reach it.

"The role of most leaders is to get the people to think more of the leader but the role of the exceptional leader is to get the people to think more of themselves." - Booker T. Washington

Personal Relationships Have More Power Than A System

"A common mistake among those who work in sports is spending a disproportionate amount of time on "x's and o's" as compared to time spent learning about people". - Mike Krzyzewski

This concept can be shared with any sport, but in my time with basketball, it was much easier to have a personal relationship with all your players. Due to the nature of having less players it is much more simple for a coach to get to know what really makes his players tick and be able to motivate them. Great football coaches are able to master this as well. It takes much more organization. Due to having so many more players with different roles and personalities it is often a very big balancing act. Coaching is all about motivating people. If we are honest with ourselves then we understand that we responded to our former coaches we knew cared about us. Take the time to get to know your athletes.

As a head football coach, this may be very difficult to do simply because of numbers on your team. I make sure to delegate much of this responsibility to my assistant coaches, but you cannot delegate this if you do not teach your assistants what you expect them to know and what to do. You cannot delegate this and not work as hard as possible to know your players, but you must use your assistant coaches to help in this area.

This was brought home to me one year, when after I chewed out a player for something, I was informed that he had been dealing with a divorce in his family. I have rarely been so humbled as a coach. Knowing your players and what is going on in their lives is the most important thing we can do as coaches. The old adage holds true, "students/players don't care what you know until they know that you care".

If you know your players well, you also know how to motivate them to reach their potential. It is easy to coach some players, but we must understand that there will be times we must coach players differently from each other. This does not mean sacrificing our values, but it does mean athletes are wired differently from each other. If we coach every player the same, we will never get them to reach their potential. I also work hard to find which assistant coach will be a better personality fit with each player. This allows the player to have a strong relationship with at least one member of the coaching staff and gives the assistant coach more ownership in the team.

As a head coach you must also have strong relationships with your assistant coaches. These guys are an extension of you, but they are not meant to be carbon copies of you. Teach them the values you want instilled in your players, but use their different personalities so that you have even more tools to reach every player on your roster. You must have a good relationship with each of your assistants if you are to be successful. I ask for 80+ hour work weeks from my guys, and if they didn't know I valued their time and their time with family, it would never work.

The next leg of having relationships is with the community. The community in which you reside needs to know that you are appreciative of all the support they give to your program. I'd highly recommend doing simple things to show appreciation: from writing thank you cards, to posting on social media, to simply calling or texting and letting them know that you value their efforts.

I do not want to delve into all the people that it takes to have a successful program in this book, but understand it is much more than just one coach. To keep the book back on pace, we will focus on working with the athletes (as they are the most important part). Just like every other part of coaching you should have the same general principles in working with athletes -

1. **Have a core set of values** that you are working to teach them to uphold. Be sure it is a clear set of values and is something they can attain. Your values are what you must decide as a coach, but they need to be clearly stated and attainable for your athletes. I would recommend making these something that has very little to do with football, but are ideals that are bigger than a game. I'd also recommend making only a small number of these and making sure

they are maintained. Too many values can be confusing. Focus on what is most important and work down.

2. **Adapt to each player** in order to help them reach the standard you have set for them. Work hard to reach them where they are, and bring them along. The goal should be to get as many players up to your standard as possible. To make this work, you must find what motivates them, and this can only be done through time and listening to your players/assistant coaches. Your goal is to bring them where you want them to go, but you must first find out how they tick. Relationships are always the key to finding great teams and coaches. Those who can motivate players will be much more successful than those who can dominate on a whiteboard, but cannot reach their players. Understand that if you were tossed away any time you failed, you would have never reached the point in life you are at now –

3. **Have patience when it would be easy to get frustrated**. I've had to put athletes off my teams more times than I wanted to, but each time I try to give them as many options as possible to stay with our team. My goal is to teach young men to become

men of character, and that means we will often hold on to them longer than we should with the hope we can save as many as possible. The consequences that I have seen from young men having nothing, keeping them in school are usually not good. Many times you are their father-figure, and take that as seriously as you can. You are responsible to the entire team, but never lose sight of why you became a coach.

4. Make sure your athletes know that you **hold yourself accountable** and be willing to admit mistakes openly and honestly. They need to know we all fail and how we deal with that failure is what will define us as people. This does not just mean in scheme or decisions in the game, although it does include these, but it means being open in how you manage people and situations. If you win, credit the players and assistant coaches, but if you lose, you take the blame.

The principle of understanding the WHY also should show up in smaller areas: Why do we clean the locker room, why do we do certain lifts, or certain drills? Players are much more likely to buy into a coach or program if they at least understand why they are doing what they are doing. And it

COACHING FOOTBALL LIKE A BASKETBALL COACH

often challenges us as Coaches to make sure we are only doing things that are pointing towards our goal.

I am a big believer in servant leadership. This is not common in the coaching profession due to it being filled with naturally competitive alpha-males. While a coach must have the respect of his players, you can accomplish much more with your team if they understand you will do whatever is needed to serve them. Athletes need to know and understand that you care for them much more than simply during practice times and games.

> *It sounds cliche, but it is the truth that the great coaches understand that players who play hard are much more important than any scheme you can draw up. This does not mean that scheme is unimportant, but if you are spending more time working scheme than you are working your core values with your players, you will not be successful. There are successful teams that run air raid, wing t and even power I. What they all have in common is they have coaches that are able to motivate and inspire great effort from their team.*

Of all the things I am proud of as a coach, the main one is watching my young men pour every ounce of effort on the field during a game. I've been as proud of them many times even when the scoreboard did not reflect what I had hoped going into a game. As much as I **like** winning games, I **love** watching young athletes lay it all on the line due to their love for each other. As a much better teacher than I once said, *"Whatever your hand finds to do, do it with all your might"* - Ecclesiastes 9:10.

Conclusion

I've been around as a head football coach now for many seasons. Some years we have had a great year, and there have been some seasons that have made me question if I even know what I am doing. As a head coach, get ready to handle the stress that comes with the position. What has made me most proud is not the "X and O's", but when I am able to visit with a young man that has graduated from our program and has gone on to do great things. Impacting the lives of young men is why most of us get into this profession.

I am hopeful some of this book can be useful to you as you continue to grow as a coach. Our profession is one of the most important professions if done correctly. The ability to impact young men that are going to become the leaders of our generation is not a task to take lightly. Be sure that you put in as much time developing your players as men of character as you do in teaching them the game of football.

While we may feel like our sport is the best game on the planet, I also hope we can recognize the other great coaches. Continue to meet with coaches of all sports who are successful in their field, and learn from them. All coaches are striving to better themselves, and the more we work across the lines with other sports, the more we can grow our coaching community. More and more I watch athletes choosing to "specialize" in sports and it makes me sad to see all the lessons they can learn from playing as many sports as possible. As coaches, I feel we must go above and beyond to show that we support other sports. Our athletes need to see that we want them to be successful on the field and on the court if they choose to do so.

One of my fears is to see the game of Football die out and my grandchildren not get to enjoy all the great lessons it can teach. I feel our game is something that will be under attack in the coming years, and hope that the next generation of coaches is able to continue to evolve the game so that it will be as great as possible. I feel football is moving in the direction of basketball with the new rules and those coaches that seem to be able to apply the principles from other sports to football are "ahead" of those who are not open minded to the new changes.

Don't let those who want to criticize you run you out of the game either. Lots of people want your job after a big win, but many don't know or want all the hours and weeks that lead up to those moments. One of my favorite quotes I tell our football players is from Teddy Roosevelt:

"It is not the critic who counts; not the man who points out how the strong man stumbles, or where the doer of deeds could have done them better. The credit belongs to the man who is actually in the arena, whose face is marred by dust and sweat and blood; who strives valiantly; who errs, who comes

short again and again, because there is no effort without error and shortcoming; but who does actually strive to do the deeds; who knows great enthusiasms, the great devotions; who spends himself in a worthy cause; who at the best knows in the end the triumph of high achievement, and who at the worst, if he fails, at least fails while daring greatly, so that his place shall never be with those cold and timid souls who neither know victory nor defeat".

I've been the "Coach of the Year" a few times by different organizations and I've been 0-10. Stay true to who you are and your core beliefs through both times, and you will show the people that matter the most to you that you are a man of character. I often tell my own children and my players that you have the choice between being a thermostat or a thermometer. The thermometer only reflects the temperature around you, while the thermostat can change what is going on. If who you are changes based on the circumstances around you, then you must re-evaluate your life.

As a coach you must decide which you are going to be, because there are only two types of coaches according to Bum Phillips... "*Those who have been fired, and those who will be fired*". If your character changes with the result of a game/season, then it is not character -- you are simply a reflection of the situation. Be the same through the winning and losing.

I've been blessed to have learned from some wonderful coaches and mentors in my time in all sports. Feel free to contact me if you have any questions. My cell is 334-549-9382 or through twitter @FbCoachSimpson. I'd love to talk and learn more about our great game. I hope this book may have given you a few things that can help you on your journey and remember that coaching is a calling, not a job. You have been born to lead the next generation of young men.

ABOUT THE AUTHOR

Coach Simpson is currently the Head Football Coach at Searcy High School, a 6A school in Arkansas. Before taking the job at Searcy, Simpson was the Head Football Coach at Southside High School, a 4A school in Arkansas. Taking over a program that had won eight games in five seasons and had been on a 20+ game losing streak, Simpson has led Southside to the playoffs for four-consecutive seasons and won two conference titles in the past three seasons. For his efforts, he was named 4A-2 Conference Coach of the Year (2017), named to the as a finalist for Hooten's Coach of the Year (2017) and has been the All-Star Nominee for the 4A-2 (2016 and 2019).

This is Coach Simpson's 4th book. He was a best-selling author for his first work Find a Way: What I Wish I'd Known When I Became a Head Football Coach. The book was released in 2019 and is available on Amazon. https://www.amazon.com/dp/1701924188. It has sold over 1800 copies as of 2020.

Simpson has also raised over $1.5 million for Southside and has overseen several major facility projects including: New Field Turf, Expansion Fieldhouse, Expansion to the school's home bleachers, and the addition of a press box and a new video-board.

Prior to coming to Southside, Simpson took over as Head Coach at Alabama Christian Academy in Montgomery, Alabama. During his tenure there, Simpson took over a team that had been 4-18 and led them to their first home playoff game in over 20-years. For his efforts he was named Montgomery Advertiser's All-Metro Coach of the Year as well as being voted 4A Region 2 Coach of the Year (2010). Simpson also served as the head track coach at ACA and led the girl's and boy's teams to multiple top 10 finishes in 4A.

Simpson began his coaching career at Madison Academy, in Huntsville, Alabama. He served as a junior high basketball and football coach, before working into a varsity coaching role in football. He graduated from Harding University in 2003. He is married to Jamey and has three children: Avery, Braden and Bennett. The couple was married in 2001 after meeting at Harding University.